SAMSUNG GALAXY S22, S22 PLUS AND S22 ULTRA 5G; AND S22 CAMERA USER MANUAL

2 BOOKS IN 1

Samsung Galaxy S22 series User manual, And Galaxy S22 Camera Guide for Beginners

Nath Jones

GW00459123

BOOK 1

BEGINNERS GUIDE TO SAMSUNG GALAXY S22, S22 PLUS AND S22 ULTRA 5G

(2022 EDITION)

A Detailed Manual to The Samsung S22 Series. Learn How to Use All the Functions and Hidden Features

Table of content

Introduction

The much-anticipated Samsung S22 series is now out. As it always is with other Samsung devices, the S22 series screams class and superior functionality.

This book is a complete manual that outlines the features of these devices, and offers a practical guide to assist you as you learn to navigate through your new device.

Let's start exploring!

Basic Layout

The Samsung S22 series comprise of the Samsung Galaxy S22, S22+ and the S22 Ultra. While the Galaxy S22 features a screen size of 6.1" in the full rectangle and 5.9" with the rounded corners taken into account, the Galaxy S22+'s offers a screen size of 6.6" in the full rectangle and 6.4" with the rounded corners taken into account. The Galaxy S22 Ultra also comes with a full rectangle screen size of 6.8". This includes the rounded corners, however the actual area of the screen that is viewable is lesser than 6.8" because the camera hole and the rounded corners are also included here.

Keys

With the screen facing upwards, there's the power button on the right-hand side of the S22 devices which offers a variety of functions including launching Samsung's Bixby voice assistant, lock screen, power off and on, restart and when combined with the volume down key, takes a screenshot. The volume keys are located right above the power button and can be used to toggle the devices' volume and activate "do not disturb" profiles.

Chapter One

S Pen

Charging the S22 S Pen

Before you using the Samsung's S Pen button in operating apps remotely, the Samsung's S Pen needs to be charged. Charging begins as soon as the Samsung's S Pen is inserted into the slot. The Samsung's S Pen will only be charged when the device is charging if the Air actions feature is turned off.

Charging

The phones in the S22 series support both wired and wireless charging. This can be done using a Samsung-approved 25W or 45W adapter or the Samsung Wireless charger. The S22 Ultra and S22+ offer 45W wired charging and 15W wireless charging, which is a significant upgrade over the previous "ultra" and "plus" variants. The Samsung Galaxy S22 series also support Wireless Power Sharing with which you can charge other Galaxy devices like phones, watches, buds, etc.

Battery optimization

Each of the phones in the S22 series offer varied battery capacities: The Samsung S22 device features a battery capacity of 3700mAh, while the Samsung S22+ phone comes with a battery capacity of 4500mAh and the Samsung S22 Ultra device has a 5000mAh battery capacity. These three devices with average usage give 54, 69 and 81 hours of music playback, respectively. However, since this is an average metric, other factors such as brightness, call time, and other utilities such as internet browsing, YouTube streaming, 3D gaming, etc., may significantly affect battery performance.

Just like other handheld devices, battery consumption of Samsung Galaxy S22 series is directly proportional to the device's processing power. This means that when extra processing power is required, more battery is consumed. Reduction in battery consumption implies reduction in features that require much processing power such as increased brightness, connections (phone signal, data, Bluetooth, Wi-Fi, and location services) and camera.

Tips for charging your phone

- If you don't have a Samsung-approved adaptor, the Fast-Charging feature may be unavailable.

- When the gadget or its screen is turned off, you can charge the battery more quickly.

- When using a conventional battery charger to charge the battery, the built-in Fast/Super-fast charging capability will not work.

- The charging speed may automatically slow down if the gadget heats up or the ambient air temperature rises. This is a typical functioning condition designed to keep the gadget from being damaged.

Quick charging

The first three times you connect a Samsung fast charger, a pop-up message will display on your phone's screen inviting you to turn on the Fast-charging option. The fast-charging feature is featured on the phones in the S22 series with the base S22 model's wired charging speed set to 25 Watts. The power used by the Qi when charging wirelessly is also set to 15W, which is the same for the entire S22 series. the Samsung S22 Ultra can charge up to 55% in just 30 minutes, using 25 Watts.

Increasing the charging rate

The rate at which the batteries in the Samsung S22 series charge can be augmented using the 45 Watts charging. With 45 Watts, the battery charges up to 66% in 30 minutes and completely charges in an astonishing 62 minutes!

Setting up your SIM or USIM

SIM cards can be placed on both the front and back of the dual SIM card tray, with the gold-colored contacts facing outwards, on Galaxy S22 Series phones that are built to accommodate two SIM cards. To install a SIM card,

- First insert the ejection pin into the hole, to release the tray
- Gently pull the tray from its slot.

- Mildly place the USIM or SIM card into the SIM card tray with the gold-colored contacts on the SIM card facing outwards.

- Replace the tray in the slot it was removed from.

Chapter Two

Activating your device

What looks to be the power button on the right-hand side (screen facing) of any S22 handset actually launches Samsung's Bixby voice assistant by default. The lock screen is accessed by pressing the button quickly. To turn off your phone, press and hold the power button and the volume down key at the same time (not a brief press, since that will merely snap a screenshot), which will bring up a software screen with options like 'Power off,' 'Restart,' and 'Emergency mode.' You can also choose 'Side key settings' from this screen to setup a long press to skip Bixby and instead bring up the power-off page.

Forcing restart

If you wish to forcibly restart your Samsung Galaxy S22, follow the procedures below:

1) Simultaneously, press down the Volume Down and Power keys.

2) Hold the buttons down for a minimum of 7 seconds.

3) Release both buttons when the phone vibrates and displays the Samsung logo.

4) If your Samsung S22 device will not switch on and you are trying to force a restart, we also consider plugging in a charger. This guarantees that the gadget receives some power and may assist in resetting the phone.

Initial setup

Setting up your new Samsung Galaxy S22 should not be a difficult process. This can be done in a few minutes. Follow the steps below to complete the first-time setup on your new Samsung device:

Setting up a Samsung account

On any of the phones in the S22 series, go to Settings.

Under accounts, select add account and then choose Samsung account. An interface to create either new or sign-in with your existing Samsung account or sign up with Google ID will be presented to you.

Proceed to select Create Account. You will be prompted to input your personal information such as email address, password, confirm password, date of birth, first name & last name.

Once you have entered all required information, accept User Terms and Conditions, then proceed to sign up.

Once completed, this should automatically sign you into your newly created Samsung account.

Login in to an already existing Samsung account

If you already have an existing Samsung account, which you would prefer to log in with on your Samsung Galaxy S22, follow these steps:

On any of the phones in the S22 series, go to Settings.

Under accounts, select add account and then choose Samsung account. An interface to create either new or sign-in with your existing Samsung account or sign up with Google ID will be presented to you.

Proceed to sign in with your existing Samsung account. Then, you'll be prompted to input your existing Samsung account information.

Once done, click sign in and your existing Samsung account will be added to your device.

Resetting your password and retrieving your identification number

Follow the procedures below to recover your Samsung ID:

1. Go to account.samsung.com from your mobile device (or PC).

2. In the upper-right corner, touch Sign In.

3. Select Forgot your Username or Password from the drop-down menu.

4. Select the Find ID option from the drop-down menu. Touch Confirm after entering the needed data.

5. Only a portion of the email address stored on file will be visible.

Follow the steps below to change your password:

1. Go to account.samsung.com from your mobile device (or PC).

2. In the upper-right corner, touch Sign In.

3. Select Forgot your Username or Password from the drop-down menu.

4. Enter the account's email address, the security code, and then click Confirm.

5. Your email address will be sent. To change your password, follow the steps in the email.

Cancelling your Samsung account

Eliminating a Samsung account is not the same as permanently deleting it. It's only temporary when you remove a Samsung account from a device; you may always add it back afterwards.

1. Swipe to Accounts and Backup from the Settings menu.

2. Choose the Samsung account on the device which you want to remove from the device from the Manage accounts menu.

3. Then, on the window, hit Remove account.

4. Sign out by tapping the X. After that, hit OK to confirm the Samsung account's password.

Data transfer (SmartSwitch)

Samsung Smart Switch allows you to move all of your data seamlessly from an old device in to a new Galaxy phone without interruption. Smart Switch can transfer data across most Android and iOS phones, as well as certain older Windows and Blackberry devices.

Transfer

Transferring your data to a new phone through wireless is the preferred method. It's quick and allows you to keep the phones charged while transferring.

- To begin, make sure both phones have the Smart Switch app installed and are plugged into their respective chargers.

- Place the phones 4 inches apart when you're ready.

- Launch Smart Switch on both devices.

- To transfer data seamlessly from the old device, go to Settings, type in Smart Switch in the search bar, and then proceed to click Bring data from the old device. Return to the old device and from there, select Bring data.

- Note: You may also launch Smart Switch from the Apps screen by tapping on the Samsung folder.

- On the old device, hit Send data and then Wireless.

External storage for data backup and restoration

Smart Switch makes it simple to move messages, photos, contacts, and other files across devices. A PC or Mac can also be used in creating a backup of files on your old device before transferring or syncing your data to your new Samsung device.

Helpful tip: For Smart Switch to function on your device, it should be running Android or iOS versions of 4.3 or 4.2.1 or later respectively.

Transferring data from a computer's backup drive

Smart Switch simplifies iCloud file transfers.

1. Open Settings, type in Smart Switch in the search bar, and then proceed to click Bring data from the old device. Return to the old device and from there, select Bring data.

2. Note: You may also launch Smart Switch from the Apps screen by tapping on the Samsung folder.

3. After that, tap iPhone/iPad and then, on the new phone, Receive data.

4. At the screen's bottom, proceed to tap Get data from iCloud.

5. Then, click Sign in to access iCloud, you will be prompted to enter your Apple ID and password.

Touch screens operations

To get started, Click Settings, Display Turn on or off the Touch sensitivity switch by tapping it Sensitivity is increased when it is turned on

Tapping

Tap your finger on the device's screen

Tapping and holding

Tap and hold your finger on the screen for roughly 2 milliseconds.

Dragging

Tap and hold an object and drag it around it to the intended recipient position.

Double tapping

Tap the screen twice.

Swiping

Swipe from the screen's bottom, descending, towards the left or right

Spreading and pinching

On the screen, make two fingers spread apart or a squeeze.

Soft Keys (The Navigation Bar)

When you switch on the device, you can find that the soft keys are at the screen's bottom. The soft keys' default settings navigate The recent, Home, and Back respectively. These functions of the soft keys may vary depending on the app in use or the environment in which they are utilized. Home screen and Apps screen

Home and Apps Screen

From the device's Home screen, you can easily start navigating and using all of the device's functions. It shows widgets, app shortcuts, and more.

All applications, —this includes applications that are newly installed— are represented as icons on the Apps panel.

You can alter the widgets, styles, wallpapers, themes and also access other settings from any home screen by pressing and holding the screen's wallpaper for a long time. Screens can also be added here. You can also erase entire screens.

Furthermore, you can also modify the screen grid's size which contain shortcuts and widgets, depending on how densely you want your screen to be arranged or appear.

Switching back and forth between Home and Apps display

If you swipe up, the Samsung S22's apps tray will be displayed from the home screen. You can then navigate the apps tray by scrolling left or right. A swipe up will also take you from the apps tray back to the Home screen.

Launching Finder

On the device, swiftly look for content.

1) Select Search from the Apps menu. To do so, open the device's notification pane, swipe downwards, and tap the search icon

2) Select a keyword from the menu presented. Your device's apps and content will be looked up.

You may search for more information by typing using the keypad.

Moving items

Drag an object to a different spot after tapping and holding it. Drag an object to the screen's side in order to move it to a different panel.

On the applications' panel, press and hold down an app icon and then tap Add to Home in order to include an app's shortcut on the Home screen. When done properly, you should find the app's shortcut on the Home screen.

Commonly used apps can also be dragged the Home screen's shortcuts section at the screen's bottom.

Creating folders

Folders are formed by simply dragging one app over another app on the home screen. Enter a folder name by tapping Folder Name.

Adding additional applications

When you want to add additional applications, simply tap and hold down the app icon, then move it into the desired folder. This can also be done using the '+' button. This way, you can also add multiple apps simultaneously from your App list. Tap and hold an app inside a folder in order to remove or uninstall it. When you do so, you will be presented with a pop-up menu allowing you to uninstall or remove it.

Tap and hold a folder in order to delete the folder. Proceed to click Delete folder. The folder would be the only thing that is removed. The programs in the folder are going to be moved to the Apps screen.

Making changes to the device's Home screen

The device's home screen's orientation as well as that of the settings, applications tray and other elements can be displayed in landscape mode. Although this setting is not enabled by default, you can enable it in Settings. Click on Home screen settings, then activate the 'Rotate to landscape orientation' option. This option is different from the Portrait/Auto rotate option available on the notification panel when you swipe down. The Portait/Auto rotate shortcut available on the notification panel only rotates selected apps between landscape and portrait orientation.

Displaying all apps on the home screen

This is a preferred alternative for most users. Tap and hold your finger on the Home screen and then tap Settings to eliminate the applications tray. Once done, go to the device's Home screen layout and select the Home screen alone option.

Indicator icons

Android's icon badges let you know how many alerts you have from each app. Samsung uses this feature across the board. You can turn off app icon badges if you do not want to see them. Do this by visiting Settings, click on notifications and turn them off in advanced settings. If you wish to switch between only a plain or numbered dot to indicate the number of notifications you may have, go to this setting.

Lock screen

When you lock your phone, the lock screen is presented. It's separated into two sections: one is shown while the screen is turned off and "always-on display" provides some information, and the other when the device's screen is completely on but the device's access is still restricted.

Modifying the manner in which the device's screen is locked

When the Samsung S22 device is locked, there's still a number of settings and features that can be toggled. To modify the manner in which the device's screen is locked, you can toggle on or off the lock screen or show a moving clock, enable the always-on layout, change the dynamics of the always-on timer, add widgets to the lock screen or even the always-on screen, change the illumination of the always-on screen, change the shortcut keys on the lock screen, and turn off or on lock screen notifications.

Notification panel

Anytime you swipe downwards on the device's home screen, the panel of notifications will drop down, so you won't have to extend all the way to the top. Swipe down once more to access the quick settings options, which are especially helpful on the Samsung S22+ as well as the S22 Ultra. You can disable this feature by

1.) Tap and hold your finger on the device's home screen

2.) Tap on the setting's icon

3.) Then scroll down to toggle the 'Swipe down for notification panel' option to either disable or enable it (it's enabled by default).

Using shortcut buttons to change settings

Using shortcut buttons to change settings is a common Android hack, but it's useful for quickly accessing settings. If you tap and hold your finger over the shortcut (for instance, Wi-Fi), you'll be taken to the entire options menu right away. It comes in handy for Bluetooth, Wi-Fi, as well as other power-saving features.

Controlling the playback of media

The media output and device control are displayed by default in the fast settings panel. This means that you can easily access your music or speakers and even control other smart home gadgets by swiping down. You can turn off this feature in the quick settings interface, if this isn't what you want, by tapping the menu in at the top right corner and toggling the switch. You can also choose your favorite option in the quick settings layout by tapping media output keys and device control.

Controlling gadgets in the immediate vicinity

The Device Panel is essentially a shortcut to each one of your smart devices that are linked to your SmartThings account or phone.

From the screen's top swipe downwards to enter the Quick panel, and then scroll downwards again to open the Device's panel.

Step 2: Under the device's Quick settings icons, tap Devices.

Step 3: Read the instructions on the device's screen and then tap Next.

Step 4: Tap Done when you're finished.

How do you capture the greatest screenshots?

Take a screenshot: Press and hold the volume down and standby buttons at the same time - but not for too long, or the power-off screen will appear.

Alternatively, you could take a screenshot when you swipe your palm's edge across the screen. To either turn this feature on or off, head to Settings, then tap on advanced features. Select Movements & gestures You can either turn the Palm swipe to capture feature on or off from there.

Screen record

The S22 device feature an in-built screen recording software which can easily be accessed through quick settings. Simply scroll downwards twice in order to reveal the entire set of 18 buttons, from there you may select Screen recorder. If you desire to modify the video and sound quality, press and hold the mic icon.

Keyboard layout

Select General management from the device's Settings menu. Toggle between Samsung Keyboard settings and Mode.

The following keyboard modes are available:

The following is a list of keyboard mode options.

Keyboard layout: This is the standard keyboard view, with the on-screen keyboard of your phone expanded to occupy the entire screen.

One-handed keyboard: The keyboard is moved to the screen's right-hand side in this mode. Tap the Left arrow symbol to move the keyboard towards the left part of the screen.

Floating keyboard: The keyboard appears as a little floating popup in the center of the screen in this mode.

Changing the language of the input

Manage input languages and choose which languages to use by going to Settings and then select Languages and Types. It is possible to switch between the selected languages when there are multiple languages selected. This can be done by swiping towards the right or left on the space bar.

Changing the keyboard

After you've downloaded a keyboard, head over to Settings and choose General management. Tap Default keyboard, then tap Keyboard list and default. Select your preferred keyboard from there.

Additional keyboard functions

Voice Typing: Samsung voice input and Google voice typing are two built-in speech-to-text apps on your phone.

Navigate to and enter Settings to enable these features.

Tap General management after pressing Keyboard list and default.

Activate the switch beside the Samsung voice input. You should also hit the switch next to any additional voice-to-text functionalities to turn them off.

Note that your phone should only have one voice assistant enabled. You may now type a message using your voice! In the Messages app, start a new conversation.

Hold down the Microphone icon in the keyboard's toolbar. When the Microphone symbol is activated, you can just talk and your words will be translated.

Press the Microphone symbol one again after you're finished.

Note: If this is your first time using Samsung voice input, you may need to accept the terms and conditions or allow some permissions.

Chapter Three

Resetting your Samsung's S Pen

If the Samsung's S Pen is having connectivity issues or disconnects frequently, reset the Samsung's S Pen and reconnect it.

In the slot, insert the Samsung's S Pen. Then tap Reset S Pen on the Air activities settings screen.

• Only Samsung-approved S Pens that enable Bluetooth Low Energy can be connected (BLE).

• When the S Pen is linked to the device, do not remove it. This will cause the procedure to be disrupted.

Command of the Air Force

Air command makes it possible for you to utilize the Samsung's S Pen's trademark features. By just removing the Samsung's S Pen from its slot, while using your phone, you can access Air command at any time. Air command can also be triggered by hovering the S Pen over the screen and then pressing the S Pen button.

You'll see a menu with various options once it's launched, including Smart choose, Screen write, and Samsung Notes. Live Messages can also be sent to family and friends, which will be a drawing that will come to life in front of their eyes. Alternatively, if you're reading a notice, article or text in a foreign language, it is possible to easily pick text with the S Pen and have it translated using the Translate tool.

Adding shortcuts to the Air command panel

Remove the Samsung's S Pen from the slot or hover it above the device's screen and tap the Samsung's S Pen button to access the Air command panel. Alternatively, you can use the Samsung's S Pen to tap the Air command icon. On the Air command panel, pick a function or app.

Removing the Samsung's S Pen will not access the Air command panel when the screen is turned off or locked with a screen lock mechanism.

In the Air command panel, click Add to add shortcuts to frequently used programs.

Samsung's S Pen characteristics

Aside from sketching, writing, and translating, the pen has capabilities like Air View, Smart Select, and Air Actions that help with productivity and efficiency.

Smart select: Capturing an area from a video

Smart Select is a screenshot-taking function that allows you to take partial or selected screenshots. Simply remove the Samsung's S Pen or press the Stylus Button on the screen to access the shortcut menu. Then go to Smart Select, which lets you drag and draw any shape on the screen to capture it. Rather to recording the entire screen and cropping it afterwards in the gallery, it is one of the simplest ways to take a screenshot. Users can also make a GIF that captures the animations in the designated area.

Screen write

Take screenshots so you can write, draw, or crop a portion of the image.

1) Open the Air command panel and press Screen write when you wish to capture something. The editing toolbar displays once the current screen is automatically captured.

2) Make a note of the screenshot.

3) The screenshot can be shared or saved.

In the Gallery, you may see the screenshots that were taken. While using some programs, taking a screenshot is not possible.

Live message

Create and send a one-of-a-kind message by capturing your activities while penning or sketching a live message and saving it as an animated file instead of sending a text message.

1) Open the Air command panel and tap Live messages when you wish to send an animated message.
2) Tap Done or Start sketching after customizing the backdrop image.
3) Use the live message screen to write or draw on.
4) Press the Done button. The live message will be saved as an animated GIF or a movie in Gallery.
5) Select a method from the Share menu.

Translate

Hover the Samsung's S Pen over the text you wish to translate to begin translating. The text's units will be transformed, as well.

1) Open the Air command panel and press Translate when you're ready to translate some text.
2) In the translator panel at the top of the screen, choose the languages you want to use. By touching or, you can switch from words to phrases.

3) Hover the Samsung's S Pen over the text or unit you'd like to convert.

The text will now be translated. Tap to hear the original text read aloud in its entirety. Depending on the language you choose, you may not see the icon.

Magnify

Try to move the Samsung's S Pen over a portion of the screen to magnify it.

Glance

To open an app in Fullscreen mode view, reduce it to a thumbnail and linger the Samsung's S Pen over it.

Making note on Calendar

Write or doodle on the calendar screen to easily and quickly fill in your plans.

Open the Air command panel, press Write on calendar, and then enter your schedule. Tap Save when you're done. Select the edit icon to make changes.

Aerial view

To preview material or view details in a pop-up window, move the Samsung's S Pen over an object on the screen.

Action buttons will appear on the preview window in some programs.

Pen select

Drag the Samsung's S Pen over text or item lists while pressing and holding the Samsung's S Pen button to pick multiple items or text. You can also share the selected items or text with others by copying and pasting them into another app.

Creating a screen off memo

Without turning on the screen, you can rapidly compose memos by scribbling on it.

Detach the Samsung's S Pen or hover the Samsung's S Pen over the screen and hit the Samsung's S Pen button when the screen is turned off.

The message will be saved to Samsung Notes if you touch Save or reinsert the Samsung's S Pen into the slot after composing it.

Using the Samsung's S Pen to unlock the screen

If the screen is locked while the Samsung's S Pen is connected, you can unlock the screen by pressing the Samsung's S Pen button.

1) Launch the Settings app and tap Advanced features → S Pen → S Pen unlock.
2) Tap Use S Pen unlock → OK.

Now you can unlock the screen by pressing the S Pen button.

• The Use S Pen unlock feature is available only when the screen lock method is set.

• To use this feature, the Samsung's S Pen must be connected to your device.XXX

Chapter Four

Bixby

Samsung's assistant is called Bixby. In 2017, it made its debut on the Samsung Galaxy S8. The virtual assistant can do a lot of things, but it's mostly divided into two parts: Bixby Voice and Bixby Vision.

Starting Bixby

Bixby will launch if you press and hold the side button. To use Bixby, you'll need to be logged into a Samsung account. You can also enable the hot word "Hi Bixby."

Awakening Bixby with your voice

If you use the "Hi Bixby" wake word, you'll be able to converse with your device in natural language, just like you would with Google Assistant. Bixby, on the other hand, appears to be prone to launching by accident, therefore employing the button press approach avoids false identification.

Communications via text

You can converse with Bixby via text if your voice is not recognized owing to noise or if you are in a scenario where speaking is difficult.

Start the Bixby app, tap, and then type your request. Bixby will also respond to you via text rather than voice during the conversation feedback.

Bixby perception

Bixby Vision makes it easier to learn more about the world around you. Bixby Vision also has accessibility support to help the visually impaired.

Launch Bixby Vision

Bixby Vision may be found in the More section of the Camera app, on the top left. This will open Vision when you tap it. Bixby Vision has a number of features that utilize the phone's camera. You may either ask Bixby what something is, or open the camera app and press the Bixby Vision button, which works similarly to

Google Lens or the Amazon buying app (in the "more" section of the app).

Recognize QR codes

Bixby Vision is configured to read barcodes and do shopping by default.

Inquiring about shopping

Tap the Vision icon in the camera or gallery app to search, shop, and translate at the touch of a finger.

Text translation or extraction

Bixby Vision is configured to read barcodes and do shopping by default, but if you open the menu, you can turn on translate, which is much more useful.

Bixby Routines

Adding routines

Bixby Routines may be found under settings > advanced features > Bixby Routines. When you click on this, you'll see a list of different routine possibilities. When traveling abroad, for example, turn off mobile data automatically. You may create custom routines based on the opening of an app, which is useful for gaming.

Adding your own routines or recommended routines

1) Tap Advanced features Bixby Routines in the Settings app.
2) Select a routine from the Discover list, or hit Add routine to create your own.

• On the Discover list, you can set the conditions and actions of routines.

• Tap Start manually to change the running condition of the program to manual. This option will only appear if no running conditions have been defined. Tap Add when a pop-up window appears. You can add the routine as a widget to your Home screen and access it instantly.

Running auto routines

When the set conditions are detected, auto routines will run automatically.

Routines that are performed manually

You can execute routines manually by touching the button whenever you want if the running condition is set to Start manually.

Tap Advanced features Bixby Routines My routines in the Settings app, then tap next to the routine you wish to run. Alternatively, tap the widget for the routine on the Home screen.

Viewing running routines

The notification panel will display the currently running routines. Tap the notice to see the specifics of a routine.

Routines can also be stopped immediately. Tap the Stop button next to a program on the notification panel.

Routines management

Tap Advanced features Bixby Routines My routines in the Settings app.

Your routines will start to show up.

To deactivate a routine, hit the More button on the routine. This routine should be disabled.

To remove routines, go to Edit, select the ones you want to remove, and then tap Delete.

Chapter Five

Making calls

1) Select Keypad from the Phone app.

2) Type a phone number in the box provided.

3) To make a voice or video call, simply tap the voice or video call icon.

Using a contact list or call log to make calls

To make a call, open the Phone app, hit Recents or Contacts, and then swipe right on a contact or phone number.

If this function isn't working, go to Settings > Other call settings and turn on the Swipe to call or text switch.

Create speed dial numbers to make calls easily

To add a phone number to your speed dial list, open the Phone app, touch Keypad or Contacts Speed dial numbers, choose a speed dial number, and then add a phone number.

To make a phone call, long press a speed dial digit on your keypad. For speed dial digits 10 and up, tap the first digit(s), then press and hold the last digit.

To make the number 123 a speed dial, press and hold 1, next tap 2, after which tap and hold 3.

Making international calls

Select Keypad from the Phone app.

2 Hold down the 0 key until you see the + sign.

3 After that, press and enter the country code, area code, and phone number.

Receiving telephone calls

To reject an incoming call, drag the green call icon outside of the circle when there is an incoming call

Rejecting an incoming call

To reject an incoming call, drag the red call icon outside of the circle when there is an incoming call.

Phone numbers are being blocked

Calls from certain numbers added to your block list will be blocked.

1 Open the Phone app and select Block numbers from the Settings menu.

2 Select contacts or phone numbers from Recents or Contacts, then hit Done.

To manually input a phone number, go to Add phone number, type the number, and then tap.

You will not be notified if a blocked number attempts to call you. In the call log, the calls will be recorded.

Incoming calls from those who do not display their caller ID can also be blocked. To use the feature, turn on the Block unknown/private numbers switch.

Contacts addition: Establishing a new contact

1 Open the Contacts app and select.

2 Decide where you want to save your files.

3 Fill in your contact information and save it.

Importing contacts

Contacts can be added to your device by importing them from other sources.

1) Open the Contacts app and select Manage contacts from the menu. Contacts can be imported or exported.

2) To import contacts, follow the on-screen directions.

Contacts are synced with your online accounts

Sync your phone's contacts with those kept in your web accounts, such as your Samsung account.

1) Open the Settings app, go to Accounts, and back up your data. Manage your accounts and choose which one you want to sync with.

2) To enable the Contacts switch, hit Sync account and then tap the Contacts switch.

Searching for contacts

Open the Contacts application. Enter search parameters at the top of the contacts list in the search box.

The contact should be tapped. Then choose proceed to do one of the following:

1) Make a telephone call.

2) Start a video conversation

3) Write a message

4) Write a message in an email.

Contacts are Shared

Using various sharing options, you can share contacts with others.

1) Open the Contacts app and select Share contacts from the menu.

2) Tap Share after selecting contacts.

3) Decide on a means of sharing.

Forming groupings

You can create and manage groups of contacts, such as family or friends.

1 Open the Contacts app and select Groups from the drop-down menu. Form a group.

2 Create a group by following the on-screen directions.

Consolidations of duplicate contacts

Merge redundant contacts into one to make your contacts list more manageable.

1 Open the Contacts app and select Manage contacts from the menu. Contacts should be merged.

2 Select the contacts you want to merge and hit Merge.

Contacts deletion

1) Open the Contacts app and select Delete Contacts from the menu.

2) Select the contacts you want to delete and tap Delete.

To delete a contact one at a time, select it from the contacts list and select More Delete.

Transmitting messages

1) Open the Messages app and select the option.

2) Enter a message and add recipients. Tap and hold, then say your message and release your finger to record and send a voice message. Only when the message input field is empty does the recording indicator appear.

3) To send a message, simply tap the send button.

View Messages

1) Tap Conversations in the Messages app.

2) Choose a contact or phone number from the messages list.

• To respond to a message, tap the message input field, type a response, and then tap.

• Spread your fingers apart or pinch the screen to change the font size.

Message classification

Messages may be sorted and managed conveniently by category.

Tap Conversations when you open the Messages app.

If the category option isn't available, go to Settings and turn on the Conversation categories switch.

Blocking unwanted text

Open the Messages app and go to Settings. You can prevent annoying communications and alter your settings.

Configuration of the message notification

Among other things, you can customize your notification settings.

Message deletion

To erase a message, tap and hold it, then tap Delete.

Chapter Six

Navigating web pages

To find information, use the Internet and save your favorite websites so you can reach them quickly.

1) Open the Internet application.
2) Tap Go after entering the web address or a keyword.
3) Drag your finger downwards on the screen to reveal the toolbars.

Swipe left or right on the address field to swiftly navigate between tabs.

Activating secret mode

You may protect your search history, browsing history, bookmarks, and saved pages by encrypting secret mode with a password.

1 Press the Secret mode button to activate it.

2 Toggle the Lock Secret mode switch to the on position, then hit Start, then enter a secret mode password.

Secret mode is turned on

The device's toolbars will change color while it is in secret mode. Some capabilities, like screen capture, aren't available in secret mode.

Secret Mode is turned off

Turn off Secret mode to deactivate it.

Etiquette while using a camera

• Do not photograph or take videos of people without their consent;

• Do not photograph or make videos where it is illegal;

• Do not photograph or record videos in situations where you may infringe on other people's privacy.

Launching camera

By default, a double touch just on side button starts the camera. If you wish to change this to, say, run another program, go to settings. Then select advanced features, next, tap Side key.

Taking pictures

Tap the image where the camera should focus on the preview screen.

Drag the adjustment bar above or below the circular frame to alter the brightness of photographs.

To take a photo, simply press the shutter button.

To switch between shooting modes, swipe left or right on the preview screen or drag the shooting modes list to the left or right.

Making use of the camera button

• To record a video, hold down the camera button.

• Swipe the shutter button towards the side of the device and keep it there to snap burst pictures.

• You can move another camera button anywhere on the screen and capture images more easily if you add another camera button. Toggle the Floating Shutter button option on the preview screen by tapping Settings Shooting techniques.

Switching between shooting modes

You are not obligated to adopt the default settings; you can add or remove modes that you find more helpful. Go to More and look for a 'Add+' at the bottom right of the screen. . If you tap that, it will be possible to bring preferred modes onto the camera's swipeable bar without having to launch More.

Choosing a camera for filming

Search and select from a list of modes on the viewfinder which is on the camera application. The default mode is Photo, next, Video. Scrolling right wards will access More and left wards will access Portrait.

Photographic mode (intelligent camera)

Capturing 8K videos: In order to capture videos in the maximum definition, head over to the Camera's video mode and tap on the aspect ratio's icon; you'll find an option for 8K 24.

Optimizer for scenes

The optimizer for scenes focuses on improving photos by using artificial intelligence (AI) while also allowing you to take longer handheld night photos. Open your camera and select the settings code in the upper left corner to toggle on 'Scene optimizer'. When you take a picture, you'll see that it auto-adjusts with a dual circular sign indicating the camera making adjustment, right before your own eyes.

Shot suggestions

This feature, which was first introduced with the S10 devices, analyzes scenes and suggests the ideal composition. When using shot suggestions, the camera will recommend the ideal shot for you and assist you in aligning it with a screen reference. This feature can be turned on by opening the device's Camera and tapping on the settings icon.

Selfies

When you have launched the device's Camera, simply slide downwards or upwards to switch between the front and back camera views. You may also switch the cameras by pressing the device's power button twice more.

Taking a portrait selfie: To do this, switch the camera's view to the front for a selfie. From the menu, select Portrait to create a portrait selfie. There's about seven various effects and backdrops to sample, which may be accessed via the small circular icon in the right corner below in the viewfinder's interface.

Filtering and beautification effects

Before shooting a picture, you can select a filter effect and alter facial attributes like skin tone and form.

79

1) Click on the preview screen to get back to the previous screen.

2) Make your selection from a wide variety of effects and snap a photo.

You can make your own filter with the My filters function by selecting a picture from the Gallery with a color tone you like.

AF (auto focus) with exposure (exposure lock) (AE)

To prevent the camera from switching its relative settings based on changes in the subjects or light sources, it is possible to lock the focus or exposure on a specific area.

To focus on an area, hold down your finger on the screen over the area you want to focus on. The focus and exposure settings will be locked after the AF/AE frame appears on the region. Even after you take a photograph, the setting remains locked.

Mode of video

Single take mode

With only one shot, you can capture a variety of images and videos.

Your device automatically chooses the best photograph and makes photos with filters or films with repeated sections.

1) Tap MORE SINGLE TAKE from the shooting modes selection.
2) Touch on the shutter button to capture the desired scene.
3) Click on the thumbnail preview, when you're finished.

Drag the icon higher to see more results. To store the results individually, press Select, check the boxes next to the items you wish to save, then proceed to select the download button.

Pro mode / Pro video mode

Manually modify several shooting variables, such as exposure value and ISO value, while taking photographs or films.

Tap MORE PRO or PRO VIDEO from the list of shooting modes. Tap to take a picture or record a video after selecting choices and customizing settings.

Divide between a focal area and an exposure area

The focus and exposure areas can be separated.

Tap and hold the preview screen wherever you want and the focus area to lock until the AF/AE lock frame appears, separates into AF and AE lock frames, and then rejoins the AF/AE lock frame. Tap and drag the AE lock frame to the desired spot for the exposure region to be locked.

Panorama mode

Take a sequence of photos in panoramic mode and then stitch them together to create a large scene.

1) Tap MORE PANORAMA on the shooting modes list.

2) Slowly tap the camera's shutter button and move the gadget in a single direction.

3) Keep the image in the camera's viewfinder within the frame. The device will automatically cease taking images if the preview image is outside the guiding frame or when you don't reposition the device.

4) Stop snapping images by touching on the screen.

Avoid using ambiguous backdrops in your photos, such as an empty sky or a plain wall.

Mode of hyper-lapse

Scenes such as passing individuals or cars can be recorded and seen as fast-motion videos.

1) Tap MORE HYPERLAPSE in the shooting modes list.

2) Select a frame rate choice with a tap. If you set the frame rate to, the device will modify the frame rate in response to the scene's changing rate.

3) Press the record button to begin recording.

4) When you're ready, tap to end the recording.

Night mode

Without using the flash, take a picture in low-light circumstances. When you utilize a tripod, your images will be brighter and more stable.

1) Select MORE NIGHT from the list of shooting modes.

You can obtain crisper visuals if you change the time on the right bottom of the screen to Max.

2) Keep tapping and holding your device firmly until the shooting is finished.

Food related mode

Food should be photographed with rich colors and fuzzy edges.

1) Tap MORE FOOD from the list of shooting modes.

2) To highlight an area, hold down your finger on the device's screen and move the circular frame over it. Outside of the circular frame, the region will be unclear or blurry. Move or adjust a corner of the circular frame to resize it.

3) If you're interested in changing the color tone, hold down your finger on the screen and move the adjustment bar.

4) Take a photo by tapping.

Changing the camera's configuration

When a camera mode has been selected, - for example, from the 'More' menu - and then wish to return to default, this might be initially confusing. You can also return to the usual viewfinder by swiping back. This would work when the gesture control is enabled; if it isn't enabled, utilize the device's back softkey to close the Camera in default photo mode.

Intelligent characteristics

Scene optimizer: Configure the device to automatically alter the color settings and apply the optimized effect based on the subject or scene.

• Suggestions for shots: Set the gadget to propose the best image composition by understanding your subject's location and angle

• Scan QR codes: From the preview screen, enable the phone to scan QR codes.

Pictures

• Swipe Shutter button to: Choose an action to carry out when you swipe the camera button to the screen's edge and hold it.

• Picture formats: Choose the format in which you want to store the image.

- Images with high efficiency: Use the High Efficiency Image Format to take photos (HEIF).

– RAW files: In pro mode, set the device to save photos as uncompressed RAW files (DNG file type). Unprocessed data from the image sensor is stored in RAW files, which can then be processed with image-processing software. They occupy up more room in the storage unit. Each image is saved in two formats when using this feature: DNG and JPG.

Videos

Set the device to automatically optimize the frame rate to record brighter movies in low-light conditions.

• Anti-shake: Enable video stabilization to decrease or eliminate fuzzy images caused by camera shake while recording a video.

• Advanced recording options: Select an advanced recording option on the device.

- Reduce file size: The High Efficiency Video Codec (HEVC) codec can be used to record videos. To save device memory, your HEVC videos will be saved as compressed files.

- HDR10+ films: You can capture videos with enhanced contrast and color for each scene.

– Zoom-in mic: You can capture sound from the zoomed-in direction at a higher volume while filming a video.

• You might now be able to play or share HEVC videos to other devices.

• The HEVC format does not support super slow motion or slow-motion videos.

• The device must support HDR10+ in order to play the HDR10+ video effectively.

Gallery
Utilizing the gallery

To use the gallery, open the gallery app.

Identical images are grouped together

Open the Gallery app and tap the group icon to categorize similar photographs together and show only the finest shots as a preview. You may see all of the photographs in the group by on the image preview.

Chapter Seven

Making films

Observing images

Select an image from the Gallery app. Swipe left or right on the screen to see different files.

Cropping photos by expanding a portion of the image

1 Open the Gallery app and choose an image to work with.

2 Tap with two fingers spread apart on the area you want to save.

A file will be created from the cropped region.

Viewing videos

Open the Gallery app and choose a video to watch. Swipe left or right on the screen to see different files.

Tap Open in Video player to get more options during playback.

Video enhancer

On an S22 device, a video enhancer is made available which is aimed at improving your video viewing experience. Prime Video, Netflix, YouTube are among the supported applications. In order to make use of this feature, head over to Settings and then click on advanced features. Select video brightness and then proceed to adjust the video's brightness. Normal and Bright are the two alternatives.

Also, it is possible to adjust the brightness by dragging your finger downwards or upwards on the playing screen's left side. To further toggle volume level, move your finger downwards or upwards on the playback screen's right side.

Creating and viewing albums

Make albums and organize your photos and videos.

To create an album, open the Gallery app and tap Albums Create album.

Moving photos and videos to albums

Select the album, then proceed to select Add items to copy or transfer the photographs or videos you wish.

Organizing albums

When you take or store photos and videos, the gadget reads their date and location markers, sorts them, and then creates stories.

Observing narratives

Launch the Gallery app, then hit Stories to find a story.

Deleting or editing narratives

Select a story and tap Add or Edit to add or remove images or videos.

Image and video synchronization

To complete the sync, open the Gallery app, hit Settings Sync with OneDrive, and then continue the onscreen steps. The Gallery app will be connected with the cloud.

When you sync your Gallery app with the cloud, all of the photos and videos you take will be saved in the cloud as well. Images and movies saved in the cloud can be seen in your Gallery app and on other devices.

When you link your Samsung and Microsoft accounts, you can choose Microsoft OneDrive as your cloud storage option.

Delete photographs or videos

To delete an image, video, or story, open the Gallery app and tap and hold it, then hit Delete.

Utilizing the recycle bin feature

You can discard the erased photos and movies. After a specified amount of time has passed, the files will be erased.

In order to enable the Trash switch or recycle bin, open the Gallery app, head over to the settings, then press it.

Launch the Gallery app and hit Trash to see what files are in the trash.

Chapter Eight

AR zone

Creating AR Emoji

It's easy to make and use your own animated augmented reality emoji, known as My Emoji. Switch to AR Emoji mode in the Camera app, then touch "Make my Emoji." Then, to design your own AR Emoji that tracks your movements, follow the instructions. With AR Emoji, you can use the animated emojis as a mask to shoot films and take selfies.

Getting rid of an emoji

To erase emojis, open the AR Zone app, tap AR Emoji Studio, tick the emojis you want to remove, and then tap Delete.

AR Emoji Camera: Capturing photos or videos with your emojis

Using various photography modes, make interesting photographs or films with emojis.

1) Open the AR Zone app and select AR Emoji Camera from the menu.

2) Choose the emoji you want to use and the mode you want to use. Depending on the emoji you choose, the available options may change.

• SCENE: The emoji tries to imitate your facial emotions. You can also modify the image that appears as the backdrop.

• MASK: The emoji's face overlays yours, giving the impression that you're wearing a mask.

• MIRROR: The emoji imitates your actions.

• PLAY: The emoji moves about on a real-world backdrop.

3) To take a picture, tap and hold the emoji icon, or to record a video, tap and hold the icon. The captured videos or images can also be viewed in the gallery.

AR Emoji stickers

Make your own stickers using the expressions and actions of your emojis. When sending messages or posting on social media, you can utilize your emoji stickers.

Making your own custom stickers

1) Open the AR Zone app and select AR Emoji Stickers from the menu.
2) Go to the top of the sticker list and tap.
3) Make whatever changes you want to the stickers and then save them.

By tapping Custom, you can see the stickers you've made.

Emoji stickers are being removed

Activate the AR Zone app and select AR Emoji Stickers. Remove all stickers. Tap Delete after selecting the emoji stickers you want to remove.

Using AR emoji stickers in Conversations

You can use your emoji stickers in a text message or on a social media platform.

The actions below demonstrate how to use your emoji stickers in the Messages app.

1) Tap the Samsung keyboard when writing a message in the Messages app.
2) Press and hold the emoji icon.
3) Choose an emoji sticker from your collection.

The emoji sticker will be placed on the card.

Deco pic

With a variety of stickers, you may capture images or movies.

Launch the AR Zone app and tap Deco Pic.

Edge screen

By providing a small menu tucked around the edge, the Edge screen was designed to make curved edges more functional. However, even though the S22 and S22+ have flat displays, they still have this feature!

Using the Edge Panels
Editing the Edge Panels

To access the edge panels, go to settings > display > edge panels. Within this, tap on Panels to get a list of available panels and to add or remove any that you don't want. Stick on the essentials; otherwise, you'll waste time navigating rather than doing.

Setting the Edge Panel handle

You can relocate the edge panel handle (where you swipe to access the edge panels) to any location on the left or right of the screen. To move it around, simply push and hold it. You can lock the location in the settings, as shown below, if you don't want to be able to move it.

Modify the edge panel handle's size and transparency: Go to Display > Edge Panels > Handle in the Settings menu. You can adjust the handle's appearance in these options, such as making it invisible, changing its color, size, and having it vibrate when it's touched.

Apps Edge

The Apps edge shows you your five most commonly used apps so you can get to them quickly.

When the smartphone is in standby mode, the edge panel functions. When the display is in standby mode, slide your finger along the edge to view the information you need, such as news updates and the weather forecast.

Editing the Apps edge panel

When you receive calls or notifications while facing down, the edge illumination feature illuminates the edge screen. You can color-code up to five contacts, who will appear in their assigned colors when they call, while all other calls and notifications will be displayed in a neutral bright light.

Multi Window

Split screen view

In split screen mode, multi window allows you to run two apps at the same time. In pop-up view, you can also launch numerous programs at once.

1.) To see a list of recently used apps, tap the Recents button.

2.) Swipe left or right to select an app's icon, then tap Open in Split Screen View.

3.) Select another app to open from the applications list.

Using the Edge panel to launch applications

Drag the Edge panel's handle to the screen's center.

Tap and hold an app, then drag it to the left and drop it where you want it. If you click here, a pop-up window will open.

The chosen app will open in a pop-up window.

Moving pop-up windows

Tap the window's toolbar and drag it to a new spot to move a pop-up window.

Samsung Notes

Creating notes

To create a note, open the Samsung Notes app, tap the plus (+) icon and then by tapping the keyboard or record icon, you can switch between input methods.

To save your note, use the Back button once you've completed writing it.

Tap Save as file if you'd like to save the note in a different file format.

Using the eraser

When erasing handwriting from a note, tap the eraser icon and pick the area you want to remove. Alternatively, press and hold the S Pen button to choose an area.

Tap once more to change the eraser type.

• Eraser stroke: Erase the line you've selected.

• Erase only the area you choose using the area eraser. By dragging the size adjustment bar, you can change the size of the eraser.

Making use of the simple writing pad

To make it easier to enter your handwriting, use the easy writing pad.

Tap on the note composer screen. The input field will be magnified and transformed into a simple writing pad.

To write or draw in your own handwriting, tap on the note composer screen.

If you magnify the screen by spreading two fingers across it, it will be easier to enter your handwriting.

Editing handwritten notes

Various editing features, such as cutting, shifting, and resizing, can be used to modify handwritten notes.

1) Tap the writing icon when there is handwriting on the note. Tap the writing icon once more to adjust the shape of the selection.

2) To choose, tap or draw a line around the input.

   • To transfer an input to a new position, pick it and drag it to the desired location.

   • Tap the input and drag a corner of the frame that appears to adjust the size of the selection.

3) Use the available options to modify the input.

Chapter Ten

Changing styles

You can modify the way you write and draw.

After you've finished writing or drawing on the screen, press twice to select a color or line thickness. Then, with the S Pen, aim it in the direction of where you wish to apply the style. When the icon displays, tap the area where you wish to make a style change.

Changing drawings into shapes

Draw a shape by tapping on the shapes icon. The scribbled shape's form will be enhanced.

Pinning a note to the Home screen

To easily view or open and edit a note, pin it to the Home screen.

1 Open the Samsung Notes app on your phone.

2 Tap Add to Home Screen after selecting a note.

The note will appear on your Home screen.

As just a reminder, save a note

You can rapidly add material to a note, such as a website link or a picture.

1 When you want to clip something while using the Internet, Messages, or Gallery apps, use the Samsung Notes app in split screen or pop-up mode. Refer to Multi window for more information on the split screen or pop-up views.

Deleting notes

To erase a note, press and hold it and then hit the Delete button.

PENUP

PENUP is a social media platform that allows users to share artwork created with the S Pen. Post your work, look at other people's work, and learn how to draw.

Start the PENUP app.

Calendar

Creating events

Launch the Calendar app and select a date by tapping or double-tapping it.

If the date already contains recorded events or tasks, tap it and then tap.

Tap Save after filling out the event details.

Establishing reminders

To begin, open the Reminder app.

2 Tap, fill in the information, and then tap Save.

Touch or select a reminder from the list of reminders, then tap Complete.

Keeping your accounts up to date with events

To sync with an account, open the Settings app, go to Accounts and backup, Manage accounts, and then select the account you want to sync with.

2 To enable the Calendar switch, hit Sync account and then tap the Calendar switch.

Launch the Calendar app and tap Options, then Settings, then Manage calendars, then the plus sign to add accounts to sync with. Then sign in with the account you want to sync with. When you add an account, a blue circle appears next to the account name.

Chapter Eleven

Music sharing

The Music Share feature allows you to share a Bluetooth speaker with another user who is already linked to your device. You can listen to the same music on both your Galaxy Buds and the Galaxy Buds of another individual.

This feature is only available on devices that have the Music Share feature enabled.

Share Bluetooth speaker

You can use your Bluetooth speaker to listen to music from your smartphone and a friend's smartphone.

1) Make sure your Bluetooth speaker and smartphone are both connected.

2) Open the Settings app on your smartphone and go to Bluetooth Connections, click Advanced, then press the Music Share toggle to turn it on. By tapping Music Share, you may access further

capabilities such as choosing who to share your device with.

3) From the list of Bluetooth devices on your friend's phone, choose your speaker.

4) Accept the connection request on your smartphone.

Your speaker's name will be revealed.

When you listen to music on your friend's smartphone, the music on your own phone is paused.

Listen to music with Galaxy Buds

You and a friend can listen to music on your smartphone through your Buds.

Only the Galaxy Buds series support this feature.

1) Make sure your Bluetooth speaker and smartphone are both connected.

2) Open the Settings app on your friend's phone, tap Connections Bluetooth Advanced, and then tap the Music Share option to enable it. By tapping Music Share, you can access further capabilities such as deciding who to share your device with.

109

3) Open the notification panel on your smartphone and tap Media output.

4) Select your friend's Buds from the detected devices list by tapping Music Share.

5) Accept the connection request on your friend's smartphone.

When you listen to music on your smartphone, both Buds can be used to listen to it.

Smart view

Connect your device to a screen mirroring-enabled TV or monitor to see your device's displayed content on a larger screen.

1) Swipe downwards to open the notification panel, then hit (Smart View).

2) To mirror your device's screen, choose a device.

Samsung DeX

On the Galaxy S22, the desktop experience (DeX) is a standard function that allows you to use your phone as a desktop computer with a PC, TV, or monitor.

Connect the device and launch Samsung DeX

To begin, go to settings > advanced features > Samsung DeX on your phone and turn on DeX. You'll either need to install the Samsung DeX software on your PC or connect the monitor to your phone via the USB-C port on the bottom once you've turned it on. USB-C hubs will also work.

Wired connection to external monitor

An HDMI adapter (USB Type-C to HDMI) can be used to connect your smartphone to an external display.

1.) Connect your smartphone to an HDMI adaptor.

2.) Plug an HDMI cable into the HDMI adapter and into an HDMI port on a TV or monitor.

3.) Press the Start button on your smartphone's screen.

The Samsung DeX screen will appear on the connected TV or monitor without modifying the screen on your smartphone.

Wired connection to computer

Connect your smartphone to a computer with a USB cord to utilize Samsung DeX.

The computer must have a USB Type-C connector to use the USB cable included with the device.

1 Download the Samsung DeX app from www.samsung.com/samsung-dex on a PC.

2 Use a USB cord to connect your phone to a computer.

3 Start now by tapping the Start button on your phone's screen.

The Samsung DeX screen will show on the computer after they have been linked.

Wirelessly connect to TV

Samsung DeX works by wirelessly connecting your smartphone to a TV or computer.

1 Open the notification panel on your smartphone, swipe downwards, and then hit (DeX).

2 On a TV or monitor, tap DeX, or on a PC, tap DeX.

3 Tap Start now after selecting a TV or computer from the detected devices list.

When screen mirroring is enabled, some TVs will only be recognized.

The PC and your smartphone must both be linked to the same Wi-Fi network.

It must be running the Samsung DeX software.

4 Accept the connection request window if it appears on the TV or computer.

5 To finalize the connection, follow the on-screen instructions.

The Samsung DeX screen will show on the TV or computer after they are connected.

• A Samsung Smart TV built after 2019 is recommended.

• Check to see if the TV you want to connect to supports screen mirroring.

Control on an external monitor

• The mouse cursor can flow from the external display to the smartphone's screen if you use a wireless keyboard/mouse. To activate the Flow pointer to phone screen switch, open the Settings app, select Advanced features Samsung DeX Mouse and trackpad, and then select the Flow pointer to phone screen switch.

• On the smartphone's screen, you can also utilize the external keyboard.

Use your smartphone as a touch pad

Open the notification panel and press Swipe gestures if the navigation bar is set to utilize them. Make a touchpad out of your phone.

• You can see the gestures you can use with the touchpad if you double-tap on it.

• If your smartphone's case includes a front cover, open it to use your phone as a touchpad. The touchpad may not work properly if the front cover is closed.

• If the screen on your smartphone shuts off, press the Side key or double-tap the screen to switch it back on.

Use the on-screen keyboard

A screen keyboard will show instantly on your smartphone's screen as you enter text to send messages, write notes, or complete other operations without having to connect an external keyboard.

Control on computer

Use the computer's keyboard and mouse to control the Samsung DeX screen.

You may drag and drop files between your computer and Samsung DeX, as well as copy and paste text.

Launch the Settings app to see what keyboard shortcuts are available while using Samsung DeX app, and then tap Keyboard shortcuts for general management

Using Samsung DeX

• Depending on the connected device, the Samsung DeX screen layout may vary.

• When you start or stop Samsung DeX, any open apps may be closed.

• When using Samsung DeX, some apps or functions may be unavailable.

• Use the display settings on the connected TV or monitor to alter the screen settings.

• Tap the status bar, select Media output, and then select a device to alter the audio output.

Using Samsung DeX and smartphone simultaneously

You can utilize separate apps on your smartphone and the external display or PC at the same time when using Samsung DeX.

For example, you can use a messenger app to talk with a friend while watching a video on the linked TV or monitor.

Launch an app for the Samsung DeX screen on the connected TV or monitor. Then, on your smartphone, open another app.

Locking Samsung DeX screen

Select Lock DeX if you wish to lock the Samsung DeX screen as well as the screen of your smartphone when using Samsung DeX.

You can't use the Side key to lock the Samsung DeX screen and your smartphone's screen while using Samsung DeX.

Transfer data with a computer

To choose a file in the My Files or Gallery applications, click and hold it on the Samsung DeX screen, then drag it to the computer screen. Drag a file from your computer screen to the Samsung DeX screen, the My Files app, or the Gallery app.

Copy and paste text

Using the keyboard shortcut keys, copy text from the Samsung DeX screen or a computer screen and paste it into the text input box on the other screen.

Link to Windows

You can connect your phone to a Windows PC to manage mobile notifications, see recent images, make and receive phone calls from your computer, access messaging/conversations, and sync mobile apps. Toggle on Link to Windows under settings > advanced features. The setup process will then begin.

Connecting to computer

Connect your smartphone to a computer with a USB cord to utilize Samsung DeX.

The computer must have a USB Type-C connector to use the USB cable included with the device.

1 Download the Samsung DeX app from www.samsung.com/samsung-dex on a PC.

2 Use a USB cord to connect your phone to a computer.

3 Start now by tapping the Start button on your phone's screen.

The Samsung DeX screen will show on the computer after they have been linked.

View data and notifications from your device on your computer

On your computer, open the Your Phone app and choose a category of notifications on your device which you would like to receive between: Messages, Photos, Apps and Calls.

Samsung Global Goals

The United Nations General Assembly adopted the Global Goals in 2015, which are a set of goals aimed at creating a sustainable society. These objectives have the potential to alleviate poverty, combat inequality, and halt climate change. Learn more about the global objectives and join the movement for a better world with Samsung Global Goals a brighter future

Google Apps

Google offers apps in the areas of entertainment, social networking, and business. Some apps may require a Google account to use.

Access the help menu of each app to learn more about it.

• **Chrome**: Use it to look for information and surf the web.

• **Gmail**: Use the Google Mail service to send and receive emails.

• **Maps**: Locate yourself on a map, search the world map, and browse location information for various locations nearby.

• **YouTube Songs**: Listen to a variety of music and watch videos on YouTube Music. You may also access and play the music collections stored on your smartphone.

• **Google** Play Movies: From the Play Store, you can buy or rent movies.

- **Drive**: Back up your files to the cloud, access them from any device, and share them with others.

- **YouTube**: View or make videos that you may share with others.

- **Photos**: All of your photos and movies from multiple sources can be found, managed, and edited in one spot.

- **Google**: Search for goods quickly on the Internet or on your device with Google.

- **Duo**: Make a quick and simple video call.

- **Messages**: Send and receive messages on your device or computer, and share various content, such as images and videos.

Depending on the service provider or model, some apps may not be available.

Settings

Make changes to the device's settings.

Open the Settings application.

Tap to find options by typing in keywords. Under Suggestions, you can also search for settings by selecting a tag.

Chapter Twelve

Connections
Wi-Fi

Connect to a Wi-Fi network and access the Internet or other network devices by turning on the Wi-Fi function.

Connect to a Wi-Fi network

1 Tap Connections Wi-Fi on the Settings screen, then tap the switch to turn it on.

2 Choose a network from the list of Wi-Fi networks.

A password is required for networks with a lock icon.

• Once connected to a Wi-Fi network, the device will automatically reconnect to that network whenever it becomes accessible, without the need for a password. To prevent the device from automatically reconnecting to the network, tap next to the network and deactivate the Auto reconnect switch. To delete the saved connection information for a network, tap next to the network and tap Forget.

• Restart your device's Wi-Fi function or the wireless router if you can't connect to a Wi-Fi network properly.

View Wi-Fi network quality information

View details about the Wi-Fi network's qualities, such as speed and stability.

Tap Connections Wi-Fi on the Settings screen, then tap the switch to turn it on. The information about network quality will appear under Wi-Fi networks. If it doesn't appear, tap it again Advanced, then toggle the Show network quality info option on.

Depending on the Wi-Fi network, the quality information may or may not appear.

Shared Wi-Fi network password

You can connect to a secured Wi-Fi network without entering the password if you ask someone who is connected to the network to share the password. This feature is available between devices that have each other's contacts, but the other device's screen must be turned on for it to work.

1 On the Settings screen, go to Connections Wi-Fi and turn on the switch.

2 From the Wi-Fi networks list, choose a network.

3 Request a password

4 On the other device, accept the share request.

Your device is connected to the network after entering the Wi-Fi password.

Wi-Fi direct

Without the use of an access point, Wi-Fi Direct connects devices directly to a Wi-Fi network.

1 On the Settings screen, go to Connections Wi-Fi and turn on the switch.

2 Select Wi-Fi Direct from the menu.

The gadgets that have been detected are listed. If the device you wish to connect to isn't listed, use Wi-Fi Direct to connect to it.

3 Select a device to which you want to connect.

When the other device accepts the Wi-Fi Direct connection request, the devices will be connected.

Select the device to disconnect from the list to end the connection.

Send and receive data

Bluetooth

Bluetooth allows you to send and receive data and media files with other Bluetooth-enabled devices.

Pair with other Bluetooth devices

1 Toggle Bluetooth on the Settings screen by tapping the switch.

A list of the devices that have been detected will appear.

2 Choose a device with which you'd like to pair.

Set the device to Bluetooth pairing mode if it isn't on the list. Consult the instructions for the other device. While the Bluetooth settings window is open, your device is visible to other devices.

3 Confirm that your gadget accepts the Bluetooth connection request.

When the other device accepts the Bluetooth connection request, the two devices will become connected.

To unpair the devices, hit the Unpair button next to the device you want to unpair.

Send and receive data

Bluetooth data transfer is supported by many apps. You can share data with other Bluetooth devices, such as contacts or media files. The actions below demonstrate how to send an image to another device.

1 Open the Gallery app and choose an image to work with.

2 Select a device to receive the photograph by tapping Bluetooth.

Turn on the visibility option for the device you wish to pair with if it isn't already visible.

3 Accept the other device's Bluetooth connection request.

NFC and payments

Your device has the ability to scan near-field communication (NFC) tags that convey product information. After downloading the necessary apps, you can use this function to make payments and purchase tickets for transit or events.

A built-in NFC antenna is included in the gadget. To avoid harming the NFC antenna, handle the gadget with care.

Read information from NFC tags

Information from NFC tags is read

To read product information from NFC tags, use the NFC function.

1 Tap Connections on the Settings screen, then turn on the NFC and contactless payments switch.

Place your device's NFC antenna region on the rear near an NFC tag. The tag's information is displayed.

2. Make sure the device's screen is unlocked and switched on. The device will not be able to read NFC tags or receive data if this is not done.

Make your payments with NFC

Using the NFC function to make payments

You must first register for the mobile payment service before using the NFC capability to make payments. Contact your service provider to register or learn more about the program.

1 Tap Connections on the Settings screen, then turn on the NFC and contactless payments switch.

2 Touch the back of your device's NFC antenna to the NFC card reader.

Open the Settings screen and select the default payment app. To change the default payment app, go to Settings > Connections > NFC and contactless payments > Contactless payments > Payment, and then choose an app.

Data saver

Reduce your data consumption by disabling some background apps from sending or receiving data.

Tap Connections — Data consumption — Data saver on the Settings screen, then tap the option to turn it on.

The data saver icon will appear on the status bar when the data saver option is enabled.

Tap Allowed to use data while Data saver is on and select apps to use data without limitation.

Mobile data-only apps

Even if your device is linked to a Wi-Fi network, select apps that will always utilize mobile data.

For example, you can configure the device to only utilize mobile data for secure apps or streaming apps that can be disconnected. The apps will launch utilizing mobile data even if the Wi-Fi functionality is not turned off.

Tap Connections — Data consumption — Mobile data only apps on the Settings screen, then tap the switches next to the apps you wish.

You may be charged more if you use this function.

Mobile hotspot

To share your device's mobile data connection with other devices, use it as a mobile hotspot.

1 Tap Connections Mobile Hotspot and Tethering Mobile Hotspot on the Settings screen.

2 To activate the switch, tap it.

On the status bar, the icon displays. By tapping Configure, you can adjust the level of protection and the password.

3 Search for and choose your device from the Wi-Fi networks list on the other device's screen.

Alternatively, you can tap the QR code on the mobile hotspot screen and scan it with another device.

• If the mobile hotspot isn't identified, go to Configure and change the Band to 2.4 GHz, then go to Advanced and turn off the Hidden network option.

• With the Auto Hotspot feature enabled, you can share your device's mobile data connection with other Samsung account-connected devices.

Other connectivity aspects can be controlled by customizing the settings.

Tap Connections More connection settings on the Settings screen.

• Scanning for nearby devices to connect to: Configure the device to search for nearby devices to connect to.

• Printing: Set up the printer plug-ins that are installed on the device. You can conduct a search.

Look for available printers or manually add one to your print files. For further information, see Printing.

• VPN: To connect to a school or company's private network, set up virtual private networks (VPNs) on your device.

• Private DNS: Configure the device to utilize the private DNS with increased security.

• Ethernet: You can utilize a wired network and configure network settings when you connect an Ethernet adapter.

Printing

Configure the printer plug-ins that are installed on the device. You can print photographs or documents by connecting the device to a printer via Wi-Fi or Wi-Fi Direct.

It's possible that some printers won't work with the device.

Add a printer plug-in

Add printer plug-ins for printers to which the device will be connected.

1 Tap Connections on the Settings screen. Tap Connections — More connection options —Printing — Install the plugin.

2 Select and install a printer plug-in.

3 Select the printer plug-in that has been installed.

The device will automatically look for printers on the same Wi-Fi network as you.

Chapter Thirteen

Biometrics and security

Biometrics aren't foolproof, as your device will revert to a PIN or password if they fail. As a result, the security of your cellphone is solely dependent on the password or PIN you employ, as anyone attempting to hack into your phone can always resort to these unlock methods.

Face recognition

You may program the device to recognize your face and unlock the screen. When you use your face as a screen lock, you won't be able to use it to unlock the screen for the first time after turning it on. To use the gadget, you must first unlock the screen with the pattern, PIN, or password you created when you registered your face. Make sure you don't lose track of your pattern, PIN, or password. All of your biometric data will be destroyed if you change the screen lock mechanism to Swipe or None, which are not safe.

Precaution on using face recognition

Keep the following concerns in mind before using facial recognition to unlock your device.

• Someone or something that resembles your image may be able to unlock your smartphone.

• Pattern, PIN, and Password are more secure than face recognition.

For better face recognition

When utilizing facial recognition, keep the following in mind: • Consider the conditions when registering, such as wearing glasses, a hat, a mask, a beard, or heavy makeup • Make sure you're in a well-lit area with a clean camera lens • Make sure your image isn't fuzzy for better match results

Register your face

Register your face indoors and out of direct sunlight for improved face registration.

138

1 Tap Biometrics and security Face recognition on the Settings screen.

2 Read the instructions on the screen and then hit Continue.

3 Determine how you want your screen to be locked.

4 Position your face within the screen's frame.

Your face will be scanned by the camera.

• If unlocking the screen with your face isn't working, tap Remove face data to delete your previously registered face and re-register your face.

• To improve face recognition, tap Add alternative appearance. This will add an alternate appearance to your profile.

Unlock the screen with your face

Using your face to unlock the screen

Instead of utilizing a pattern, PIN, or password, you can unlock the screen with your face.

1 Tap Biometrics and security Face recognition on the Settings screen.

2 Use the default screen lock technique to unlock the screen.

3 Toggle the Face unlock switch on or off.

4 Look at the screen on the locked screen.

You may unlock the screen without utilizing any additional screen lock methods after your face is detected. Use the preset screen lock technique if your face isn't recognized.

Delete registered face data

You have the option of deleting any registered facial data.

1 Tap Biometrics and security Face recognition on the Settings screen.

2 Use the default screen lock technique to unlock the screen.

3 Remove facial data by tapping Remove.

All associated features will be removed if the registered face is deleted.

Fingerprint recognition

Your fingerprint information must be registered and retained in your device for fingerprint recognition to work.

For better fingerprint recognition

• Depending on the service provider or model, this functionality may or may not be available.

• Fingerprint recognition improves the security of your device by recognizing the unique properties of each fingerprint. It's quite unlikely that the fingerprint sensor will mix up two separate fingerprints. However, in rare circumstances where two fingerprints are strikingly similar, the sensor may mistake them for one and the same.

• A thick protective covering can have a negative impact on performance. If you're going to use a screen protector, make sure it's listed as compatible with the on-screen fingerprint sensor (like Samsung's screen protectors).

• If you use your fingerprint as a screen lock, you won't be able to use it to unlock the screen for the first time after turning it on. To use the device, you must first unlock the screen with the pattern, PIN, or password you created when you registered your fingerprint. Make sure you don't lose track of your pattern, PIN, or password.

• If your fingerprint isn't detected, use the pattern, PIN, or password you set when registering the fingerprint to unlock the device, and then re-register your fingerprints. If you don't reset the device after forgetting your pattern, PIN, or password, you won't be able to use it. Samsung is not liable for any data loss or inconvenience incurred as a result of forgotten unlock codes.

• All of your biometric data will be destroyed if you change the screen lock mechanism to Swipe or None, which are not safe.

Register your fingerprint

Go to settings > biometrics and security to unlock with your fingerprint or face. You can use this page to register your face or fingerprint (or multiple prints). To offer additional security, you'll need to create a backup PIN or password at the same time.

Top tip: if you're using fingerprints, make sure to register each hand's fingers so you can unlock your phone no matter how you're holding it.

1 Tap Biometrics and security Fingerprints on the Settings screen.

2 Read the instructions on the screen and then hit Continue.

3 Determine how you want your screen to be locked.

4 Place your finger on the fingerprint sensor to activate it. Lift your finger up and place it on the fingerprint recognition sensor once again after the gadget detects it.

Carry on in this manner until the fingerprint has been registered.

Tap Done when you're through registering your fingerprints.

By tapping Check added fingerprints, you may see if your fingerprint has been registered.

Unlock the screen with your fingerprint

Instead of utilizing a pattern, PIN, or password, you can unlock the screen with your fingerprint.

1 Tap Biometrics and security Fingerprints on the Settings screen.

2 Use the default screen lock technique to unlock the screen.

3 To activate the Fingerprint unlock switch, tap it.

4 Place your finger on the fingerprint identification sensor on the locked screen and scan your fingerprint.

Change fingerprint recognition icon settings

When you tap the screen while the screen is turned off, set the device to show or hide the fingerprint recognition symbol.

1 Tap Biometrics and security Fingerprints on the Settings screen.

2 Use the default screen lock technique to unlock the screen.

3 When the screen is off, tap the Show symbol and choose an option.

Deleting registered fingerprints

You can erase fingerprints that have been registered.

1 Tap Biometrics and security Fingerprints on the Settings screen.

2 Use the default screen lock technique to unlock the screen.

3 Tap Remove after selecting a fingerprint to erase.

Chapter Fourteen

Samsung Pass

When utilizing services that require your login or personal information, register your biometric data with Samsung Pass and easily prove your identity.

• The website sign-in option is only available if you use the Internet app to view the website. This feature may not be available on all websites.

• Your biometric information is solely saved on your device and is not shared with other devices or servers.

Sign up for Samsung Pass

Register your biometric data with Samsung Pass before using it.

Tap Biometrics and security Samsung Pass on the Settings screen. To finish the setup, follow the on-screen directions.

Verify Samsung account password

When purchasing material from Galaxy Store, for example, you can use your registered biometric data to prove your identity instead of entering your Samsung account password.

Toggle the Verify with Samsung Pass switch on the Samsung Pass main screen by tapping Settings Account and syncing.

Sign in to websites with Samsung Pass

You can effortlessly sign in to websites that allow ID and password autofill with Samsung Pass.

1 On the website's sign-in page, enter your ID and password, and then touch the sign-in button.

2 When a pop-up box displays, asking if you want to save your sign-in data, select Sign in with Samsung Pass and then hit Remember.

Sign into the app with Samsung Pass

You can effortlessly sign in to apps that enable ID and password autofill with Samsung Pass.

1 Enter your ID and password on the app's sign-in screen, then hit the app's sign-in button.

2 When a pop-up box opens asking if you want to save your sign-in credentials, select Save.

Manage login information

Manage your sign-in information for the websites and apps you've set up to use Samsung Pass.

1 Tap Apps or Websites on the Samsung Pass main screen, then choose a website or app from the list.

2 Edit your ID, password, and the name of the website or app by tapping Edit.

Tap Delete to remove your sign-in information.

Use Samsung Pass via website and app

You can quickly sign in with Samsung Pass when using websites or apps that allow it.

Tap Apps or Websites on the Samsung Pass main page to see a list of websites or apps that support Samsung Pass.

• Depending on the service provider or model, the websites and apps available may vary.

• Samsung is not liable for any loss or inconvenience incurred as a result of using Samsung Pass to sign in to websites or apps.

Automatically enter your personal information

On apps that enable autofill, you can use Samsung Pass to quickly enter personal information such as your address or payment card details.

1 On the Samsung Pass main screen, go to the Private details section and choose an option.

2 Fill in the information and save it.

When inputting personal information automatically on supported apps, you can now use the biometric data you registered with Samsung Pass.

Delete your Samsung Pass data

You can erase your Samsung Pass biometric data, sign-in information, and app data.

Tap Settings to see all Samsung Pass-enabled devices on the Samsung Pass main screen. • Exit Samsung Pass. Your Samsung account will continue to function normally.

• Samsung Pass data on other Samsung devices that are logged in to your Samsung account will be removed as well.

Secure folder

You can utilize the Secure Folder if you're concerned about others having access to your phone and discovering information they shouldn't.

Secure Folder secures your personal information and apps, like as photos and contacts, from prying eyes. Even when the device is unlocked, you can keep your private content and apps safe.

A Secure Folder is a distinct, password-protected storage space. Secure Folder data cannot be shared with other devices via unauthorized sharing methods like USB or Wi-Fi Direct. Secure Folder will be immediately locked and unavailable if you try to change the operating system or modify software. Make a backup copy of the data in another secure location before saving it in Secure Folder.

Setting up your secure folder

You may then add files, photographs, and programs that you wish to keep concealed - anything from personal photos to business data - and this adds another degree of protection. You can also add additional safe and private versions of programs. It's in the biometrics and security > secure folder section of the settings menu.

1 Tap Biometrics and security Secure Folder in the Settings app.

2 To finish the setup, follow the on-screen directions.

The Secure Folder screen will show, along with the Secure Folder app icon () on the Apps screen. Tap Customize to modify the name or icon of Secure Folder.

• You must unlock the Secure Folder app using your preset lock method when you first use it, and you can reset your Secure Folder unlock code using your Samsung account if you forget it. Enter your Samsung account password by tapping the button at the bottom of the locked screen.

Set auto-lock conditions for secure folders

Setting a requirement for Secure Folder

1.) Automatically lock Launch the Secure Folder app and select Settings Auto lock Secure Folder from the menu.

153

2 Select a lock option from the drop-down menu.

Tap Lock and leave to manually lock your Secure Folder.

Add application

In Secure Folder, add an app to use.

1 Open the Secure Folder app and press the plus icon.

2 Tap Add after selecting one or more apps installed on the device.

Delete the application from the secure folder

To delete an app, tap and hold it, then tap Uninstall.

Moving content to a secured folder

Place content in the Secure Folder, such as photos and videos. The steps below demonstrate how to move a picture from default storage to Secure Folder.

1 Open the Secure Folder app and go to Files > Add.

2 Touch Images, then tick the images you want to relocate and tap Done.

3 Press and hold the Move button.

The items in the original folder will be removed and relocated to Secure Folder. Tap Copy to copy stuff.

Depending on the type of content, the process for transporting it may differ.

Add account

Accounts to be added

Sync your Samsung and Google accounts, as well as other accounts, with Secure Folder's apps.

1 Open the Secure Folder app and go to Settings, Manage Accounts, then Add Account.

2 Choose a service for your account.

3 Complete the account setup by following the on-screen prompts.

Hiding safe folder

From the Apps panel, you may hide the Secure Folder shortcut.

To deactivate the Add Secure Folder to Apps screen option, open the Secure Folder app, press Settings, and then hit the Add Secure Folder to Apps screen switch.

Alternatively, to deactivate the feature, open the notification panel, swipe downwards, and then press (Secure Folder). If (Secure Folder) isn't listed on the fast panel, press and drag the button over to add it.

To activate the Add Secure Folder to Apps screen option, go to the Settings app, hit Biometrics and security, Secure Folder, and then tap the Add Secure Folder to Apps screen switch.

Uninstalling or unmounting secure folder

Secure Folder, as well as its content and programs, can be uninstalled.

Tap Settings > More settings > Uninstall in the Secure Folder app.

Tick Move media files out of Secure Folder and select Uninstall to back up content before uninstalling Secure Folder. Launch the My Files app and tap Internal storage Download Secure Folder to access files backed up by Secure Folder.

Saved notes in Samsung Notes will not be backed up in any way.

Secure Wi-Fi

Secure Wi-Fi is a Wi-Fi network connection security service. It encrypts data transmitted over Wi-Fi networks and blocks tracking apps and websites, allowing you to safely utilize public Wi-Fi networks. When you use an unsafe Wi-Fi network in a public location, such as a cafe or an airport, Secure Wi-Fi is immediately activated, ensuring that no one can access your login information or track your activities on apps and websites.

Tap Biometrics and security Secure Wi-Fi on the Settings screen, then follow the on-screen instructions to finish the configuration.

The icon will appear in the status bar when Secure Wi-Fi is enabled.

• Using this function may cause your Wi-Fi network to slow down.

• Depending on the Wi-Fi network, service provider, or model, this feature may or may not be available.

Choose apps that use secure Wi-Fi protection

Choose which apps to secure with Secure Wi-Fi so that sensitive information, such as your password or app activity, is safe from prying eyes.

Tap Biometrics and security Secure Wi-Fi Settings on the Settings screen.

Tap the switches next to the apps you wish to protect using Secure Wi-Fi under Protected apps.

This functionality may not be available in all apps.

Buying protection program

Every month, you will receive a free Wi-Fi network protection plan. You can also buy premium protection plans that provide you unlimited bandwidth protection for a set period of time.

1 Tap Biometrics and security Secure Wi-Fi on the Settings screen.

2 Tap Protection is a method that uses two taps to protect you. Upgrade and choose your preferred plan.

You can transfer specific protection plans to another device that is signed in to your Samsung account.

3 To finish the transaction, follow the on-screen instructions...

Book 2

SAMSUNG GALAXY S22 CAMERA USER GUIDE

SAMSUNG GALAXY S22 CAMERA USER GUIDE

A Beginners Manual to Master All Camera Features of Samsung Galaxy S22, S22 Plus, And S22 Ultra, And Take Professional Photos and Videos: Including Camera Tips and Tricks

By
Nath Jones

INTRODUCTION

The new Samsung Galaxy S22 series has been the rave since its released. A lot has been said and written about this power smartphone: its new processor, gorgeous design, and truckload of features and functionalities. What has had little coverage though is the cameras.

I mean, it's no secret that the Samsung flagship devices come with some of the most powerful cameras in the smartphone industry. But just how much more powerful the Galaxy S22 series, particularly S22 Ultra's camera is, has not been explored fully.

This user manual seeks to fix that. The content herein focuses on the Samsung Galaxy S22 series cameras; with special interest placed on the S22 Ultra.

This is not to say that you will be left out if you have any of the other devices in the series (S22 and S22 Plus). On the contrary, this book contains sufficient information required to enable all S22 series users master the use of all the cameras on their device.

There is a high chance that you are under-using the cameras in your smartphone. Not to worry though, by the time you are done studying this user guide, you will be able to perform all possible functions with your device cameras, and take breathtaking pictures.

This manual carefully explores all features and offers an understandable guide for you to navigate through your Samsung S22's Camera seamlessly.

Let's get right to it!

CHAPTER ONE

Rear Camera Capacity

The rear camera setup includes:

- 12MP Ultra-Wide Camera
- Pixel size: 1.4μm
- FOV: 120°
- F.No (aperture): F2.2
- 1/2.55" image sensor size
- 2x50MP Wide-angle Camera
- Dual Pixel AF, OIS
- Pixel size: 1.0μm (12MP 2.0μm)
- FOV: 85°
- F.No (aperture): F1.8
- 1/1.56" image sensor size
- 3x10MP Telephoto Camera
- Pixel size: 1.0μm
- FOV: 36°
- F.No (aperture): F2.4
- 1/3.94" image sensor size

Space Zoom

3x Optical Zoom

Super Resolution Zoom up to 30x

Selfie camera capacity

- 1x10MP Selfie Camera
- Dual Pixel AF

1) Pixel size: 1.22μm
2) FOV: 80°
3) F.No (aperture): F2.2
4) 1/3.24" image sensor size

CHAPTER TWO

How to use Galaxy S22 camera quick launch

When you complete your purchase, you can unbox your brand-new Galaxy S22. This will reveal your sleek device. The device's side key will open the camera app almost immediately when you press it twice. That's how to activate the camera quick launch on your Galaxy S22. Other Samsung Galaxy devices using One UI as well as most Android devices have this feature.

You'll find the side key on the right side of your device. Press it twice for the camera quick launch even without unlocking your device.

When you perform the camera quick launch without unlocking your device, it will only be possible to view photos that you take during the current session. Other photos on the devices will not be accessible until you unlock your device. This also happens when you click on the camera icon from the lock screen. This is only a security measure.

How to Enable or Disable Galaxy S22 Camera Quick Launch

On the Galaxy S22, the camera quick launch feature is switched on by default. When the camera doesn't launch after performing the quick launch steps, it means that the feature is turned off.

Launch Settings from the device's Application screen or Home screen. You can also launch settings from the quick settings panel by clicking on the Settings icon.

Proceed to click on Advanced features. From here, you can personalize different features on your device. Select the camera quick launch and touch the side key.

You can customize the Side Key function with two gestures. Double press and long press.

The Side key's double press gesture is set to activate or deactivate the camera quick launch.

CHAPTER THREE

Taking A Picture

To take a picture, open the Camera application from the App drawer or Home Screen.

It is important to note that:

❖ When you perform the camera quick launch without unlocking your device, it will only be possible to view photos that you take during the current session. Other photos on the devices will not be accessible until you unlock your device. This also happens when you click on the camera icon from the lock screen. This is only a security measure

❖ The camera application will shut off automatically when it is not in use.

❖ Depending on your device model or service provider, some features won't be available.

Click on the subject in the preview screen to set the camera focus.

5) Tap and move the adjustment bar which appears below or below the circular frame in either direction. This will adjust the picture's brightness.

6) Click on the circular frame to take a photo.

7) Change the shooting mode by dragging the shooting modes list rightward or leftward. Alternatively, you can swipe rightward or leftward on the preview screen to toggle the shooting mode.

Click on the white shutter icon at the middle bottom part of the screen to take a photo.

❖ Depending on which shooting mode is set and camera in use, the preview screen will have different outlays.

❖ When the subject is too close to the camera, the focus may not be clearly visible. It is ideal to take the videos or photos from a good distance.

❖ Try cleaning camera lens if the pictures or videos appear blurry when shooting.

- Ensure that the device's lens is not contaminated or damaged, if not, the device won't function properly with high resolution modes.

- The Galaxy S22's camera has a wide-angle lens feature. With this, it is not abnormal to find minor distortion occurring in wide-angle videos or pictures. This does not necessarily translate into a dysfunctional device.

- The resolution in use will determine the maximum capacity for video recording.

- When there is a sudden change in the air temperature, it is possible for the camera to form condensation. This is because of the different temperatures inside the camera cover and outside it. You can try to avoid this when you want to use the camera application. Let the camera dry naturally before shooting videos or taking pictures to avoid blurriness from fogging.

How to Take Selfies

It is possible to take selfie portraits using the device's front camera.

3) Click on the rotate icon at the bottom right corner to toggle between the front and rear camera.

4) Hold up the camera to your face and stare into the front camera lens. Click on the wide-angle icon to take wide-angle shots of people or the landscape.

5) Click on the camera icon to take a photo.

Applying Filter and Beauty Effects

It is possible to modify the features of your face like your face shape, and skin tone before you take a picture. You can also choose a filter effect.

- Touch the wand icon at the top right corner on the preview screen.

- Proceed to choose effects and then take a photo.

With the My Filters feature, it is possible to generate your unique filter with an image's color tone you like from your device's gallery.

Shot Suggestions

The device's camera automatically suggests what composition would be ideal for your picture by recognizing the angle and position of the subject.

3) Touch the settings icon on the preview screen and then proceed to toggle the Shot Suggestions either on or off.

4) Select Photo on the shooting modes list.

   A pop-up guide should be visible from the preview screen.

5) Position the guide at the subject. The device's camera will then recognize the image's composition and recommend a composition on the preview screen.

6) Try moving the device around to help the guide match the composition recommended. The guide

will switch to a yellow color when the ideal composition is being achieved.

Touch the camera icon to take a photo.

How to Use the Camera Button

Touch and hold down the white shutter icon in order to record a video.

You can take burst shots by swiping the camera button to the screen's edge and then holding it.

It is possible to take pictures conveniently when you can click the shutter icon from anywhere on the device's screen. To activate this feature, click on Shooting Modes and toggle the Floating Shutter button switch either on or off.

How to Use Zoom in Features

You can choose .6/1/3/10, move it to the right or left to zoom out or in. Also, you can pinch two of your fingers on the screen to zoom out, and spread out both fingers to zoom in. A zoom guide will be visible on your device's screen to show what part of the image you are

173

zooming in on. This only happens when the zoom ratio has exceeded a particular level.

1. 6: The Ultra-wide camera will allow you to record wide angle videos and take wide angle pictures of various subjects such as landscapes.

2. 1: The wide-angle camera makes it possible for normal and basic pictures or videos to be taken or recorded.

3. 3: You can enlarge the subject when taking pictures or recording videos with the telephoto camera (3x).

4. 10: You can enlarge the subject when taking pictures or recording videos with the telephoto camera (10x).

CHAPTER FOUR

Portrait Mode / Portrait Video Mode

With the Samsung S22 camera, you can capture videos or pictures with a blurred background and the subject standing out very visibly. It is possible to add a background effect which you can edit after snapping a picture.

3) Click on Portrait or Portrait Video under More in the Shooting Modes list.

4) Touch background effect and choose the background effect you'd prefer. Move the adjustment bar's slider when you want to adjust the background effect's intensity.

5) Click on the shutter icon or the record button to snap a picture or record a video respectively whenever you're ready.

❖ Depending on the mode of shooting, some options may or may not be available.

❖ This feature is ideal in an environment with adequate light.

❖ In certain conditions which will be listed below, the background blur feature may not function optimally. They include:

a) When the subject or device is in motion.

b) When the subject is transparent or thin.

c) When the background has a similar color to the subject.

d) When the background or subject is plain.

Pro   Mode   /   Pro   Video   Mode
You can record videos or take pictures and tweak different shooting options like ISO and exposure values simultaneously.

Click on More and then select Pro or Pro Video on the shooting modes.

Choose options and then proceed to personalize the settings.

Then you can click on the shutter icon or the record button to snap a picture or record a video respectively whenever you're ready.

Available options

1) **Settings Reset**

2) **ISO**: Choose an ISO value. This feature controls the camera light sensitivity. High values are used for dimly-lit or fast-moving objects while low values are used for brightly-lit or static objects. However, it is important to note that using high values for ISO settings could result in noisy photos or videos.

3) **SPEED**: Control the speed of the shutter. With a slow shutter speed, greater amounts of light is allowed in, thereby making the videos or picture brighter. This setting is best for taking videos or pictures taken at night or of scenery. Conversely, a quick shutter speed permits lesser amounts of lights while recording videos or taking pictures. This setting is best for taking pictures or recording videos of fast-moving subjects.

4) **EV**: Switch or toggle the exposure value. The exposure value controls the amount of light received by the camera's sensor. When there's not much light, it is ideal to use an exposure value that is high.

5) **FOCUS**: Adjust the focus mode. Move the adjustment bar's slider when you want to adjust the focus.

6) **WB**: Choose an adequate white balance so that recorded images or pictures possess a true-to-life color range. It is possible to adjust the color temperature.

7) **MIC**: Choose the direction you would want to record its sound at a higher level. It's also possible to use a Bluetooth Microphone or USB by connecting it to your device.

8) **ZOOM**: Set the zoom speed (Pro video mode).

Recording High-Resolution Pro Videos

Record high-resolution pro videos with a maximum resolution of 8K.

1. Click on FHD (30) and then swipe the top panel to the right. You should find 8k (24) at the top left corner, click on it to record a pro video.

2. When you're done recording a pro video, you can play it using the Gallery application. When you click on a frame that you prefer, this frame will be saved as a high-resolution picture.

CHAPTER FIVE

Separating the Focus Area and the Exposure Area

Using the steps below, it is possible to separate the focus/ exposure area.

1) Click and hold down the preview screen.
2) Automatically, the AF/AE frame would be displayed on the screen. Move the frame towards the area which you want to separate the focus area and the exposure area.

How to Activate Tracking Autofocus

Auto focus makes it possible to quickly lock in on a chosen point or area in a bid to prejudice sharper images

- Launch the Camera app.
- Open Photos by swiping
- Tap your finger on an area on the screen and then click on the auto focus icon to switch on Auto Focus.

- Touch the capture button to take a picture when you're ready.
- Captured picture will be available for viewing in the Gallery Application.

How to Activate Night Mode

In dimly-lit conditions, you can take pictures without using the camera's flash light. With a tripod, you will get even steadier and brighter pictures.

1) Click on More and then select Night on the shooting modes. You may have clearer photos when you set the time that is displayed on the screen's right bottom.
2) Click on the shutter button and steadily position your device until you are done shooting.

CHAPTER SIX

Food Mode

Use vibrant colors when taking pictures of your meals.

1) Click on More and then proceed to select **Food** on the shooting modes list.

2) Touch the screen and then move the circular frame to the area you want to highlight. When you do this, the area that is outside the circular frame will become blurred. You can resize the circular frame by dragging a corner of the frame.

3) Click and move the adjustment bar to set the color tone.

4) Proceed to click on the shutter icon to take a picture.

Hyper-Lapse Mode

Shoot scenes like moving cars and people and then view them as quick-motion videos.

1) Click on More and then proceed to select Hyper-lapse on the shooting modes list.

2) Touch the frame rate icon to choose a frame rate option. The Galaxy S22 will automatically set the frame rate to match the changing rate of the scene if you select it.

3) Touch the record icon to being recording.

4) Touch the stop button to complete recording.

How to Use the Bokeh Effect While Taking Pictures

1) Launch the Camera application

2) Proceed to select the Live Focus mode.

3) Set the blue intensity to your preference with the adjustment bar displayed on your screen.

4) Take the picture immediately you achieve the blur effect that you want.

CHAPTER SEVEN

How to Use the Face Effects

You can use the face effects feature to eliminate red eye, make your eyes appear bigger and even brighten the tone of your skin.

4) Launch the Gallery application and then choose the picture that you want to edit.

5) Touch the Edit icon and the click on the three dots for more options. When you do that, proceed to click on Face Effects.

6) It is possible to choose from a wealth of editing alternatives. These options include red eye fix, tone and smoothness.

7) When you tap on an option, adhere to the recommendations that would appear on your screen. Alternatively, you can move the slider to set your preferred intensity. In example, spot fixer will help you to eliminate face blemishes when you click on certain areas of the person's face. You can use the arrows to redo or undo your edits

8) Click on Done when you have finished editing.

9) Should you need to start over, you can click on Revert and then click on Revert to Original.

10) Click on Save and then touch Save again to save your newly-edited photo to your device. Maintain the original picture on your device by clicking on the three vertical dots to open More options. Proceed to click on Save as copy to keep the original picture.

Panorama Mode

With the Panorama mode, you can take multiple pictures and then join them together to create a picture with wide scene.

1) To use this feature, open More and then select Panorama on the Shooting modes list.

2) Touch the shutter button and then slowly move the phone in one direction.

Maintain the image inside the frame on the camera's viewfinder. When the preview image is not inside the guide frame, or stop moving the device, the camera will stop taking the pictures automatically.

3) Touch the Stop icon to stop taking pictures.

Try to not take pictures of indistinct backgrounds like a plain wall or an empty sky.

Single Take Mode

Snap different pictures and videos with just one shot.

The Galaxy S22 will select the best shot automatically and create pictures with videos or filters with certain sections repeated.

1) Click on More and then select Single Take on the shooting modes list.

This should open up the Single Take Mode.

Click on the icon at the top right corner to choose what kind of images to capture in the single take mode. Click on an option to select or deselect it.

2) Touch the shutter icon when you want to capture a particular scene. This should begin a timer.

3) Touch the preview thumbnail to see the result when you are done.

You can see other results by dragging the widget upwards. Individually save the results by clicking on Select and then ticking the items you would like to save. Then proceed to click on the arrow facing down.

CHAPTER EIGHT

Super Slow-Mo Mode

The Super slow-mo is one feature that helps you to efficiently record a quickly-passing moment slowly in a way you can appreciate later.

4) Click on More and select Super Slow-Mo in the shooting modes list and then click on the record icon to record a video. The device will record the moment in a really slow motion and then save it on your device as a video.

5) Click on the preview thumbnail on the preview screen to see your video.

6) Touch the pencil icon and move the section editing bar to the right or left in order to edit the super slow-mo video.

It is ideal to use this feature in an environment with sufficient lighting. If you record a video indoors with poor lighting or insufficient light, the device's screen may appear grainy or dark. The device's screen can flicker in certain lighting conditions like environments with fluorescent lighting.

Recording   ***Super***   ***Slow-Motion***   ***Videos***
Automatically

You can record videos in a really slow motion automatically. This will record videos once motion detected in the motion detection area. Touch the icon to activate it. The motion detection feature will be turned on and the motion detection area will be displayed on the preview screen.

1) Touch the record icon to begin recording. When motion has been detected, the camera will begin recording in a really slow motion. Your video will also be saved onto your device automatically.

Super Slow-mo recording may begin at a wrong time when any of the following conditions are is present:

The device shakes or another object moves near the subject that is in the motion detection area.

Recording in certain lighting conditions like environments with fluorescent lighting.

Slow Motion Mode

Capture a moment to view it in slow motion. It's possible to appropriate the parts of your video you want to be played I slow motion.

1) Click on More in the shooting modes list and then select Slow Motion. Next click on the record icon to start recording a video.

2) Click on the square stop icon to stop recording.

3) Touch the preview thumbnail on the preview screen to view your video.

The video's quick segment will be turned into a slow-motion section, and the video will begin to play. Based on the footage, up to two slow motion portions will be made.

You can edit the slow-motion section by clicking on the pencil icon and then dragging the section editing bar to the right or left.

CHAPTER NINE

Video Mode

Automatically, the camera will adjust the shooting options depending on the environment. This is to record videos easily.

1) Click on Video on the shooting modes list and the touch the record icon to begin recording a video.

   a) You can switch between the rear and front camera while you are recording by swiping down or upwards. Alternatively, you can touch the rotate icon to switch cameras.

   b) You can also take a picture from the video while you are still recording. Touch the Camera shutter icon to do this.

   c) You record a sound from a particular direction more by pointing the camera in that direction and then adjusting the zoom.

2) Touch the Stop icon to finish recording your video.

   o The video quality may deteriorate in order to stop the device from overheating when you use the video zoom feature for a long time.

o   In dimly-lit environments, the optical zoom feature may not work.

How to Add Background Music to Video

1) Open the video that you would like to edit. It is possible to find any video by either opening the Gallery or launching the Camera application on your device.

2) Click on the edit option. Typically, this option is found below the video when you open it from the preview mode in the Gallery application.

3) Proceed to click on Movie Maker. This should take automatically to the Samsung Galaxy Store App. Here, you can easily download and install the Samsung Movie Maker app.

4) Touch install and proceed to download and install the movie maker on to your device.

5) Launch the Movie Maker. With the Movie Maker now installed, you can now access more video editing features by launching it.

6) Click on the plus sign (+) icon. You will find this gray button at the bottom-right corner of your device's screen. Clicking on it will pick a new video for editing. Depending on the video editing app you may be using, this option may differ.

7) Choose the video you would want to edit. After opening the menu for choosing a new video, click on the icon for the folder that contains your saved video and then select Done to upload it to Movie Maker.

8) In the Template menu, click on Custom. It will then be possible to add a template to your video when you upload it. Select Done to open the basic video editor menu.

9) Click on the white plus (+) icon that appears on the bottom-left of the video editor. This will allow you to add new elements to your video.

10) Click on the Audio Tab. This will bring up the menu that will allow you to add audio to your video include. This includes any music that you may have saved on your device.

11) Choose your preferred music for your video. With the menu for adding audio open, you can navigate and select any music file on your device to add to your video.

12) Set the audio volume. Scroll downwards in the editing menu on the screen's right side to reveal the Volume option. This is represented by a speaker icon. Touch it to bring up the master volume controls.

13) Proceed to save your video. With the music you added synced to with your video, you can now press Save on the screen's left side in the main video editing menu. Choose where you prefer to save it to and watch it later.

How to Combine Multiple Video Clips into One

- Launch the Gallery app.
- Navigate to the video you would like to include in your project.

- Touch the edit button at the bottom left corner of the device's screen. It should look like a pencil.

- Click on Add at the screen's top and then select a second video to combine with the first video. It is possible to select still images and multiple clips and then click on Done when you are ready. Locate one of the videos you want to include in your project.

CHAPTER TEN

How to Add Effects During Video Call

This changes or edits the background when you are making a video call. This feature also blocks background noise during video calls.

Click on Advanced Features on the Settings screen and then select Video call effects.

Touch the switch to toggle it on or off. The icon will be visible when you are making a video call on the video calling apps screen.

Viewing Brighter and Clearer Videos

Improve your videos' image quality in order to enjoy more vivid and brighter colors.

Open Settings app and then click on Advanced features. Proceed to click on Video Brightness and then select Bright.

• This feature is only available in some apps.

• Using this feature may cause your device's battery to drain quickly.

How to View Videos

Open the Gallery all and choose a video you would like to play. You can swipe right or left on the screen to see other files.

Touch the three vertical dots at the bottom right corner of the screen and then select Open in Video Player to use more options during video playback.

Dragging your finger upwards or downwards on the left part of the playback screen will adjust the brightness. Dragging your finger upwards or downwards on the right part of the playback screen will adjust the volume.

You can fast-forward or rewind the video by sliding your finger horizontally on the screen either to the left or right side.

CHAPTER ELEVEN

Using Video Call Effects

Click on the video icon on the screen of the video calling app. Click on:

4) **Reset all:** To reset the entire video call settings to default.

- **Background**: To blur or change the background during video calls.

- **Auto framing**: Deactivate or activate the auto framing feature. This feature enables the device to change the zoom and shooting angle automatically why tracking and recognizing people during a video call when it is activated.

5) **Mic mode**: This ensures clearer sound by blocking background noise.

– **Standard**: Removes all noise so that it sounds just as a normal voice call.

– **Voice focus:** Focuses on the sound coming from the direction of the front camera.

– **All sound:** Transmits the entire sounds around you like the sound of other people, background music.

- **Settings**: Add or select images or background cookies to be in use during video calls.

It is important to note that:

Depending on the device model, most features won't be available.

Most features will only be available when the front camera is in use.

Screen Capture

Take a screenshot when you are using the device. You can decide to draw or write on it. You can also decide to crop or share the screenshot. It is possible to capture the scrollable area and current screen.

Screenshots can be viewed in the Gallery application. To take a screenshot, follow the instructions below:

Hold the volume down key and the side key down simultaneously. This will take a screenshot. This is the Key Capture method.

Alternatively, you can use the swipe capture method. This would require you to swipe your hand across the screen either leftward or rightward.

There are some apps and features that would restrict you from taking a screenshot.

You may need to activate the swipe capture method, if the swipe capture method does not take a screenshot. To activate it, open Settings and click on Advanced features. Proceed to click on Motion and gestures and then select the Palm swipe to capture feature to activate it.

When you finish taking a screenshot, you can perform a number of functions with it using the toolbar at the screen's bottom. These functions include:

1) Capture an entire page (like a webpage), both the part visible on the screen and the part not visible. When this is done, the screen will automatically swipe downwards to screenshot the rest of the page not in view.

2) Draw or write on a captured screenshot. You can also crop a part out of a captured screenshot. The cropped part will be available for viewing in you Gallery app.

3) Include tags to your captured screenshot. You can search for screenshots using the tags. Click on Search at the top area of the Apps Screen and then select Screenshots. It is possible to see the tags list and easily sort for the screenshot you are looking for.

4) Share your captured screenshot with others.

If these functions are not readily visible from the captured screen, open the Settings app and then touch Advanced Features. Click on Screenshots and Screen recorder and then select the Screenshot toolbar switch to switch it on.

CHAPTER TWELVE

How to Use the Screen Record

Make a recording of your screen while you are using your device.

1) Launch the notification panel, scroll downwards and then touch the screen recorder icon to activate it.

2) Choose a sound setting and then click on Start Recording. A countdown will begin, after which your recording will start.

   You can write or draw on the screen by selecting the pencil icon

   You can record your screen with a video overlay of yourself by clicking on the icon.

3) Click on the Stop icon when you are done with your recording.

   Your screen record will be available for viewing in the Gallery app.

   Change the screen recorder settings by opening the settings app and then clicking on Advanced Features. Select Screenshots and Screen recorder.

Capturing an Area from a Video

While a video is being played, you can choose a portion of the video and capture it as a GIF animation.

If you have a content that you would like to capture during a video playback, simply:

1) Open the Air command panel and then click on Smart Select.
2) Touch GIF on the toolbar
3) Set the size and position of the area you want to capture.
4) Click on Record to begin capturing.
   a) Before capturing a video, you should make sure that the video is playing.
   b) The maximum capturing duration will be shown on your device screen.
   c) If you are capturing an area from a video, the sound will not be recorded.
5) To stop capturing, click on Stop.
6) Choose an option to use with the chosen area.

a) You can either draw or write on it. Click on the pencil icon to do this. Tap the play button to see the finished project before proceeding to save the file to your device.

b) Click on the share icon to share the area you have selected with others.

c) Use the arrow facing downwards to save your file onto your device.

Stabilizing Videos (Super Steady)

You can put this feature to use when there is a lot of shaking while you are recording a video.

Click on Video on the Shooting Modes List and then select the Shooting options to activate the video stabilization feature. After this, you can record a video.

Utilize the auto framing feature and adjust the device to change the zoom and shorting angle automatically by tracking and recognizing people while recording videos.

Click on Video in the Shooting modes list and the touch shaky hand icon to activate it. After this, you can record a video.

It is possible to track and adjust the shooting angle as well as zoom in on a particular individual. To do this, just click on the frame that is displayed around the person. You can deactivate the tracking feature by clicking on the frame again.

CHAPTER THIRTEEN

How to Turn on 8K Video Capture

Record videos in the highest possible resolution.

Launch the video mode from inside the Camera app.

Proceed to click on the aspect ratio icon and then you will see the 8K 24 option.

How to Use scene optimizer to improve your photos:

The scene optimizer makes use of artificial intelligence (AI) in improving your pictures. It also allows longer handheld night photos.

1) Open the Camera app and then click on the settings icon at the top left part of the screen.

2) Proceed to switch the Scene optimizer on

3) Snap a picture and then you will notice that it auto-adjusts using a dual circular icon to indicate that the camera has made optimization.

How to Extract High Resolution Image from a Video

You can take still images from video Galaxy 22.

1) Launch the Samsung Video player app or open the Gallery.

2) Navigate to the video which you would like to take a photo from.

3) Begin playing the video and then click on the Quick crop icon at the screen's bottom left corner.
   Move the video's duration bar to the point where you would like you capture your image.

4) The preview image will be visible at the screen's bottom left corner.

5) You can open the Gallery app to find the picture you captured by searching the Video Captures folder.

CHAPTER FOURTEEN

Capturing an Area from a Video

Chose a portion of a video that you would like to capture as a GIF animation.

If you have a content that you would like to capture during a video playback, simply:

1) Open the Air command panel and then click on Smart Select.
2) Touch the capture icon on the toolbar
3) Set the size and position of the area you want to capture.

How to Edit the Available Camera Modes

Remove or add modes that are more essential.

1) Click on More and you will find and "Add +" visible at the screen's bottom right

2) Touch it and then you will be allowed to move the modes you want onto the swipe-able bar. After this is done, you will not need to open the More section to find modes to select.

How to Quickly Switch from Rear to Front Camera

1) Open the Camera app and then drag your finger upwards or downwards to easily switch between the back and front camera views.

2) Alternatively, double pressing the power button will also toggle between the front and rear camera views.

CHAPTER FIFTEEN

How to Shoot in HDR10+ Video

The Galaxy S22 can shoot in HDR10+ video. However, this feature is still in its Beta or Labs stage.

4) Launch the Camera app and open Settings.
5) Click on Advanced recording options and you will see the options available for the High Dynamic Range Capture format, however, it is only available when you are shooting 1080p30.

How to Enable Raw Capture

This feature saves pictures like a regular JPEG. To use this feature,

6) Launch the camera app and then click on Settings at the screen's top left corner
7) Proceed to click on Picture Formats.
8) You will see the available options to save Raw copies. Toggle the switch on or off.
9) You can also switch the High Efficiency pictures ((HEIF) on as well.

How to Resize Photos

4) Launch the Gallery App and then choose the picture that you would like to resize.

5) Click on the Edit icon at the screen's bottom.

6) Proceed to select the More options which are the three vertical dots at the screen's top right corner.

7) Click on Resize

8) Select your preferred resized image percentage from the resize image options and then click on Done to apply your changes.

9) Click on Save when you have finished editing.

CHAPTER SIXTEEN

How to Enable Voice Commands on Galaxy S22 Camera App

1) Unlock your phone and click on the Camera apps icon once. Alternatively, you can open the camera from the App drawer.

2) Touch the Gear icon at the top left corner of your screen

3) Navigate through your Camera's settings and click on Shooting methods.

4) Click on the Voice commands toggle in order to activate it. When this is done, you will not be able to start recording videos or click on images using just the S22 voice commands.

How to Use the Auto Framing Feature

1) Launch the camera app from the App drawer on your device and then click on Video.

2) Touch the Auto Framing icon at the bottom corner of your screen to switch the feature on.

3) The icon will give a yellow beam once the feature has been turned on.

   Begin by holding your device a good distance away from the subject to enable them to be seen visibly by the camera. Click on Record to to start filming.

   You will find that once a new subject gets within the viewfinder, the camera will begin following them while still focusing on the original subject.

4) When you are done filming, click on Stop to finish.

What are Samsung Galaxy S22 Voice Commands

The voice command feature makes it possible for the device owner to make a video or take pictures using preset commands.

The S22 devices have the following voice commands compatible with them:

- Capture

- Smile
- Cheese
- Shoot
- Record Video

CHAPTER SEVENTEEN

Customizing Camera Settings

Depending on the shooting mode, most options will not be available when you click on the Settings icon from the preview screen.

Intelligent Features

- **Scene optimizer:** This feature sets the Galaxy S22 to control color settings and apply the optimized effect automatically depending on the scene or subject.

- **Shot suggestions:** This feature enables the Galaxy S22 to recommend a composition that would be ideal for your picture. This is done by recognizing the subject's angle and position.

- **Scan QR codes**: Allow the Galaxy S22 to scan QR codes from the preview screen.

- **Swipe Shutter button to**: Choose a function to be performed when you swipe the camera button to the screen's edge and hold it.

Pictures

- **Picture formats**: Choose the format you would like to save your picture with.

- **High efficiency pictures:** Snap photos with the High Efficiency Image Format (HEIF).

- **RAW copies:** Adjust the Galaxy S22to save photos as uncompressed RAW files (DNG file format) with pro mode. RAW files retain a picture's entire data and gives the best quality. They will, however, consume more space. With the RAW copies feature in use, every picture is saved in two formats — DNG and JPG.

Selfies

• **Save selfies as previewed**: Adjust the Galaxy S22 to download pictures the way they appear on the preview screen when taken with the front camera without flipping them.

• **Selfie color tone:** Choose a tone to apply for taking selfies.

Videos

• **Auto FPS:** Adjust the Galaxy S22 to record brighter videos even with dimly-lit environment by optimizing the frame rate automatically.

• **Video stabilization:** Enable anti-shake in order to eliminate or reduce blurry image as a result of camera shake during video recording.

• **Advanced recording options**: Allow the Galaxy S22 to make use of an advanced recording option.

– **Reduce file size:** It is possible to record videos with the High Efficiency Video Codec (HEVC) format. In order to save space on your phone's memory, the HEVC videos that have been recorded will be stored as compressed files.

– **HDR10+ videos**: It is possible to record videos each scene optimized in color and contrast.

– **Zoom-in mic**: It is possible to record sound at a higher volume from a zoomed-in direction while you are recording a video.

• It may not be possible to share the HEVC videos online or play them with other devices.

• You will not be able to record slow motion and Super slow-motion videos in the HEVC format.

• The device should support HDR10+ in order to play the HDR10+ video efficiently.

General

• **Auto HDR:** Snap photos using bright and vibrant colors and highlight details even in dark and bright areas.

• **Tracking auto-focus:** Adjust the Galaxy S22 to track and focus on a highlighted subject automatically. Even when the subject is in motion or th camera's position is changed, the camera will still focus on the subject as long as the subject has been selected on the preview screen.

However, there are certain conditions in which tracking a subject may not be successful. These conditions include when the subject is:

> ➢ Too small or too big
> ➢ Is not steady or is in motion
> ➢ Is back-lit or in a dimly-lit environment
> ➢ Shares colors or patterns with the background
> ➢ Possesses horizontal patterns like blinds.
> ➢ Is steady but the camera is shaky.

In situations where the video resolution is high or the optical zoom is used to zoom in or out, the subject tracking may also not be successful.

• **Grid lines:** This feature shows viewfinder guides in an attempt to help composition during subjects' selection.

• **Location tags:** Include a GPS location tag to the picture.

• In locations where the signal is obstructed like in low-lying areas, in-between buildings, or in environments

219

with poor weather conditions, the GPS signal strength may decrease.

• To avoid your location from being visible when you upload your photos on the internet, disable the location tag setting.

• **Shooting methods**: Choose additional shooting methods for recording a video or taking a photo.

• **Settings to keep:** Keep the previously used settings when you open the camera like the shooting mode.

• **Vibration feedback:** Adjust the Galaxy S22 to vibrate in certain conditions like when you click on the camera button.

How to Configure the Shooting Method

1) Click on the Camera icon at the lower right corner of the screen on the Home Screen page.

2) Alternatively, you can swipe upwards or downwards with a finger from the middle of the display and then click on Camera.

Click on the Settings icon and then select Camera Settings in the upper left part of the screen to open general Camera settings.

Swipe to the right or left in order to navigate through the options that are available from the Camera screen.

Select an option in order to either turn Switch on icon on or off:

- Voice commands
- Floating Shutter button
- Show palm

CHAPTER EIGHTEEN

How to Create/Decorate an AR Emoji Short Video

You can make a short video using an emoji which can either be used as a call background image or a wallpaper.

4) Open the AR zone app and then click on AR Emoji Studio

5) Click on Create video. Select either Call screen or Lock screen.

6) Choose a template that you prefer. You can click on the gallery icon to modify the background image.

7) Click on Save to store your video file on your device. You can assess the saved videos in the Gallery.

8) Choose an option at the screen's bottom to use the video directly.

AR Emoji Camera

This feature makes fun videos or pictures using emojis in different shooting modes.

1) Open the AR zone app and then click on AR Emoji Camera.

2) Choose the emoji and mode that you would like to use. The modes that are available may vary depending on which emoji you choose.

• **SCENE**: The emoji mimics your expressions. You can also change the background image.

• **MASK**: The emoji's face appears over your face so it looks like you are wearing a mask.

• **MIRROR**: The emoji mimics your body movements.

• **PLAY**: The emoji moves on a real background.

3) Click on the emoji icon in order to take a picture or touch and hold your finger over the icon to record a video.

It is possible to assess and share the videos and pictures you have captured from the Gallery app.

How To Activate AR Doodle

Create funny videos of people or pets with virtual handwritings or drawings on their faces or anywhere else. When you do this, they do doodle will follow a face that has been recognized as it moves. The doodles that have been created will remain in the same position even when the camera moves.

1) Open the AR Zone and click on AR Doodle. The recognition area will be visible on the screen once the camera recognizes the subject.

2) Touch the pencil icon to write or draw in the recognition area. You can also draw or write outside the recognition area when you switch to the back camera.

   If you click on the rotate icon and then start doodling, you can record yourself as you doodle.

3) Click on the record icon to record a video

4) Touch the Stop icon to end the video recording.

   The created video can be viewed or shared from the Gallery. Depending on which camera is in use, the available features on the preview screen may vary.

Albums

Make albums and organize your videos and images.

Open the Gallery app and then click on Albums. Touch the three vertical dots and then select Create album. This will create an album.

Once created, select the album and then proceed to add items by clicking on Add Items. You can then move or copy the videos or pictures you want to the album.

Stories

Anytime that you save or capture videos and images, the Galaxy S22 will read their location tags, date and organize the videos and images and then make stories with them.

Open the Gallery all and then click on stories. Proceed to choose a story.

You can delete or add videos or images by selecting a story and then clicking on the three vertical dots. You can then proceed to tap add or edit.

Syncing Images and Videos

Open the Gallery app and click on the three horizontal lines, then proceed to select settings. Click on Sync with OneDrive and then you follow the instructions that will appear on your screen to finish the sync process. The Cloud and the Gallery app will be synced.

With the Gallery synced with the cloud, videos and pictures taken will also be saved onto the cloud. You can assess the videos and pictures that are saved in the cloud in your Gallery as well as from other devices.

When you connect your Samsung account and Microsoft account, you can set the cloud storage as Microsoft OneDrive.

CHAPTER NINETEEN

Deleting Images or Videos

Open the Gallery app and then click on the three horizontal lines and hold your finger over an image, story or video to delete it and then click on Delete.

Using the Recycle Bin Feature

Deleted videos and pictures can be kept in the recycle bin. These files will be removed once a certain period of time has elapsed.

Open the Gallery app and then click on the three vertical lines. Touch Settings and the click on the Recycle bin switch to turn it on.

You can view files that are in the recycle bin by opening the Gallery, clicking on the three vertical dots and then select the Recycle Bin.

Cropping Enlarged Images

Open the Gallery app and then choose a picture.

Place two finger on the image and spread them apart over the area that you want to save and then tap crop icon.

This will save the cropped portion as a file.

CHAPTER TWENTY

Motions and Gestures

Enable the motion feature and configure settings.

Click on Advanced Features and then select Motions and Gestures.

5) **Lift to wake**: Make the Galaxy S22 to automatically turn on the screen when you pick it up.

3) **Double tap to turn on screen**: Make the Galaxy S22's screen to turn on when you double-tap anywhere on it while it is turned off.

- **Double tap to turn off screen:** Make the Galaxy S22's screen to go off when you double tap anywhere on it while it is turned on.

- **Keep screen on while viewing:** Make the Galaxy S22's display always on while you are looking at it.

- **Alert when phone picked up**: Make the device notify you once you have new messages or missed calls as soon as you pick up the device.

This feature may not work if the screen is turned on or the device is not on a flat surface.

3) **Mute with gestures**: Silence with gestures: Use motions or gestures to mute certain sounds on the device.

4) **Palm swipe to capture:** The photographs recorded can be viewed in the Gallery. While utilizing specific programs and functionalities, taking a screenshot is not available. Excessive shaking or an impact to the device may cause an unintended input for some features using sensors.

How to Increase the Timer in Night Mode

The Night Mode analyzes the scene in front of the camera by default and adjusts the shutter speed accordingly.

1) Go to Night Mode and press the Timer icon in the lower-right corner.

2) Choose "Max" and press the Shutter button.

How to Erase Shadow and Reflection on Galaxy S22

This feature removes undesired reflections and shadows.

3) Use Samsung Gallery to open the image you want to edit.

4) Select the three-dot menu from the drop-down menu.

5) Select Labs. Turn on the Share Eraser and Reflection Eraser toggles now.

6) Return to the previous screen and select Object Eraser.

7) Click the Erase Shadows or Erase Reflections button after drawing around any shadows or reflections you want to remove from the image.

CHAPTER TWENTY- ONE

How To Activate Voice Command

1. To get started, go to the Home screen or the Apps viewer and select Settings.

This brings up the main Settings menu.

2. In the Settings menu, scroll down to Apps and tap it. On the next screen, a list of all installed and downloaded applications will appear.

3. To access the camera app's features and options, look for and tap Camera.

To continue, tap Camera settings.

5. Scroll down the following menu and select Shooting methods.

On the next screen, various shooting methods for the Camera app will be displayed.

6. Toggle the switch next to Voice commands to turn it on.

This activates voice commands for taking pictures and recording movies with the phone's default camera app.

Bixby
Introduction

Bixby is a user interface that helps you use your device more conveniently.

Samsung's assistant is called Bixby. In 2017, it made its debut on the Samsung Galaxy S8. The virtual assistant can do a lot of things, but it's mostly divided into two parts: Bixby Voice and Bixby Vision.

Starting Bixby

Bixby will launch if you press and hold the side button. To use Bixby, you'll need to be logged into a Samsung account. You can also enable the hot word "Hi Bixby."

Using Bixby

Awakening Bixby with Your Voice

If you use the "Hi Bixby" wake word, you'll be able to converse with your device in natural language, just like you would with Google Assistant. Bixby, on the other hand, appears to be prone to launching by accident, therefore employing the button press approach avoids false identification.

Communications Via Text

You can converse with Bixby via text if your voice is not recognized owing to noise or if you are in a scenario where speaking is difficult.

Start the Bixby app, tap, and then type your request. Bixby will also respond to you via text rather than voice during the conversation feedback.

You can talk to Bixby or type text. Bixby will launch a function you request or show the information you want. Visit www.samsung.com/bixby for more information.

Bixby is only available in some languages, and it may not be available depending on the region.

Bixby Vision

Bixby Vision is a service that makes it easier to learn more about the world around you. Bixby Vision also has accessibility support to help the visually impaired.

Launch Bixby Vision

Bixby Vision may be found in the More section of the Camera app, on the top left. This will open Vision when you tap it. Bixby Vision has a number of features that utilize the phone's camera. You may either ask Bixby what something is, or open the camera app and press the Bixby Vision button, which works similarly to Google Lens or the Amazon buying app (in the "more" section of the app).

Alternatively, you can launch Bixby Vision using these more ways:

• In the Gallery app, select an image and tap.

• In the Internet app, tap and hold an image and tap Search with Bixby Vision.

• If you added the Bixby Vision app icon to the Apps screen, launch the Bixby Vision app

Using Bixby Vision

1. Open Bixby Vision.

2. Choose a feature which you would like to use.

Using the camera, Bixby Vision can:

4) Recognize QR codes: Using the camera, Bixby Vision is also configured to read barcodes and do shopping by default.
5) Inquire about shopping: Tap the Vision icon in the camera or gallery app to search, shop, and translate at the touch of a finger.
6) Recognize text from documents or images and extract it.

236

7) Search for images similar to the recognized object online and related information.

The available features and search results may vary depending on the region or service provider.

How to Use the Quick Share

Content sharing with neighboring devices. Share content with adjacent devices using Wi-Fi Direct or Bluetooth, as well as SmartThings-compatible devices.

1. Open the Gallery app and choose a photo.

2. Open the notification panel on the other smartphone, swipe downwards, and then tap (Quick Share) to activate it. If (Quick Share) isn't visible on the quick panel, press + and drag the button across to add it.

3. Select a device to send the photograph to by tapping Quick Share.

4. On the opposite device, accept the file transfer request.

This functionality does not allow you to share videos with TVs or other SmartThings devices. Use the Smart View feature to watch videos on TV.

SmartThings

With your smartphone, you can control and manage smart appliances and Internet of Things (IoT) gadgets.

To learn more, open the SmartThings app and go to Menu > How to use.

1. Open the SmartThings application.

2. Select Add device or + from the Devices menu.

3. Follow the on-screen steps to select a device and connect to it.

• Depending on the type of connected devices or shared material, several connection techniques may be used.

• Depending on your location, the devices you may connect may differ. The functionality available may vary depending on the linked device.

• The Samsung warranty does not cover the faults or defects of connected devices.

Contact the maker of the connected devices if issues or faults occur.

How to Use the Smart Select

Smart Select is a screenshot-taking function that allows you to take partial or selected screenshots. Simply remove the Samsung's S Pen or press the Stylus Button on the screen to access the shortcut menu. Then go to Smart Select, which lets you drag and draw any shape on the screen to capture it. Rather to recording the entire screen and cropping it afterwards in the gallery, it is one of the simplest ways to take a screenshot. Users can also make a GIF that captures the animations in the designated area.

CHAPTER TWENTY -TWO

Accounts and Backup Options

Samsung Cloud allows you to sync, back up, and recover the data on your smartphone. You can also use Smart Switch to login in to accounts like your Samsung or Google account, as well as transfer data to and from other devices.

Tap Accounts and backup on the Settings screen.

• Manage accounts: Sync with your Samsung and Google accounts, as well as other accounts.

• Samsung Cloud: Back up your data and settings and restore the data and settings of your previous device even if you don't have it. For additional information, go to Samsung Cloud.

• Google Drive: Back up your personal data, app data, and device settings to Google Drive. You can make a backup of your important data. To back up data, you must sign in to your Google account.

• Launch Smart Switch to transfer data from your prior device. For further information, see Transferring data from your old device (Smart Switch).

Back up your data on a regular basis to a secure location, such as Samsung Cloud or a computer, so you can recover it if it is corrupted or lost due to an unexpected factory data reset.

Restoring Data

Restore your backup data from Samsung Cloud to your device.

1 On the Settings screen, tap Accounts and backup.

2 Tap Restore data and select a device you want.

3 Tick items you want to restore and tap Restore.

How To Reset Camera Settings

The camera application settings on the Samsung Galaxy S22 Camera can be reset to their default levels.

To reset the camera application's settings, follow these steps:

1. Launch the camera app and select >

2. Select Settings.

3. Select General.

4. Choose Yes and Reset.

This choice will only reset the camera application's settings. It will have no effect on the Galaxy Camera's operating system settings, and it will not delete any of your personal data from the camera.

About Director's View Mode on Galaxy S22

Record videos with various angles of view by changing cameras. In this mode, both the subject and the person who is filming can be recorded at the same time.

1 On the shooting modes list, tap **MORE** **→DIRECTOR'S VIEW**.

2 Select the screen and the camera thumbnail you want and tap ⊙ to record a video.

> 4) To change the screen before starting the recording, tap and select the screen you want.
>
> 5) You can change the camera thumbnail while recording. If the thumbnail is hidden, tap ⊚ to display it.

3 Tap ☐ to stop recording the video.

Privacy

Privacy Notice: View the privacy notice.

• **Permissions**: View the permissions required to use the Camera app.

• **Reset settings**: Reset the camera settings.

• **About Camera**: View the Camera app version and legal information.

Printed in Great Britain
by Amazon

14552034R00139